Germany

Text by Mike Ivory
Edited by John Mapps
Picture Editor: Hilary Genin
Series Editor: Tony Halliday

Berlitz POCKET GUIDE

Germany

First Edition 2006

PHOTOGRAPHY CREDITS

akg-images London 19, 21, 111; Berlin Tourismus Marketing (BTM)/Koch 29; Bodo Bondzio 46, 82; Siegfried Bucher 16; Chris Coe/Apa 30, 39, 104, 105, 108, 113; Andreas Gross 15, 140; Tony Halliday/Apa 28, 31, 33, 35, 37, 40, 106, 110, 112, 133; Bildagentur Huber 100, 131; Bildagentur Huber/Alfeld 125/ F. Damm 58, 70, 128/ S. Damm 50/ Giovanni 78/ Gräfenhain 13, 42, 73,74, 90, 93, 94, 97, 148/ Klaes 91/ Krammisch 10, 55, 77/ Mehlig 52/ Müller Stauffent 138/ R. Schmid 2BL, 6, 9, 51, 62, 67, 98, 99,103, 115, 116, 117, 119, 120, 121, 123, 126, 127, 136, 143, 145/ Szyszka 1, 61, 68/ B. Radelt 3TL, 85/ Zoom 24; Landesbildstelle Berlin 22; Robin Laurence/Apa 48, 49; Bildarchiv Monheim 44, 53, 57, 64, 65, 80, 81, 86, 87, 89; Mark Read/ Apa 134; Phil Wood/Apa 107, 147

Cover picture: Digital Vision/Robert Harding Picture Library

CONTACTING THE EDITORS

Every effort has been made to provide accurate information in this publication, but changes are inevitable. The publisher cannot be responsible for any resulting loss, inconvenience or injury. We would appreciate it if readers would call our attention to any errors or outdated information by contacting Berlitz Publishing, PO Box 7910, London SE1 1WE, England.
Fax: (44) 20 7403 0290;
e-mail: berlitz@apaguide.co.uk
www.berlitzpublishing.com

Cologne Cathedral, one of the greatest Gothic churches of Christendom (page 81)

Mad King Ludwig's fantastical castle of Neuschwanstein is Germany's most popular visitor attraction (page 114)

Rothenburg-ob-der-Tauber is one of the most perfectly preserved medieval towns in Europe (page 126)

TOP TEN ATTRACTIONS

The Branden-
burg Gate, the
enduring
symbol of
Berlin
(page 28)

The Rhine Valley, at its most
dramatic in the gorge to the south
of Koblenz (page 91)

The pristine waters of the Königsee
are overlooked by the Watzmann, one
of the highest peaks of the Bavarian
Alps (page 117)

Sanssouci Palace and park, the
centrepiece of Prussia's royal city,
Potsdam (page 40)

The spectacular rock
formations of Saxony's 'little
Switzerland' region south of
Dresden (page 60)

Munich's Alte
Pinakothek,
one of the
world's great
art galleries
(page 111) ➤

The Deutsches Museum in
Munich, a treasure house
of science, technology and
invention (page 112) ➤

CONTENTS

Fact Sheets

INTRODUCTION

With 83 million inhabitants, the Federal Republic of Germany *(Bundesrepublik Deutschland)* is the most populous country in the European Union and one of the largest, covering an area of 357,000 sq km (138,000 sq miles). Some of its frontiers are formed by natural boundaries such as the North Sea and Baltic to the north, and the Alps to the south. Elsewhere the borders are less well defined in a geographical sense: in the east, the same rather featureless landscape of the North European Plain continues on both sides of the border with Poland; in the west a stretch of the Rhine is shared with France. The Rhine flows into the Netherlands through the flat and watery countryside common to both countries, while in the southeast, the wooded Ore Mountains and Bavarian and Bohemian forests are shared with the Czech Republic. In the west, Germany, Belgium and Luxembourg merge almost imperceptibly in the green uplands of the Ardennes.

Today's Germany

Germany remains the economic powerhouse of Europe. Its industrial products are second to none, its towns and cities are linked by a superlative network of *Autobahnen* and high-speed railway lines, and its people continue to enjoy one of the world's highest standards of living. The reunification of the country in 1990 was accomplished peacefully, and billions have been spent on bringing the infrastructure of former East Germany (GDR) up to Western standards. Nevertheless, deep differences in attitude continue to distinguish East and West Germans from one another, with many easterners *('Ossis')* resenting westerners as pushy and superficial, and

Detail of the Franconia statue in front of the Residenz, Würzburg

westerners ('Wessis') looking down on easterners as compla-
cent and lacking in initiative. And other persistent problems
continue to plague the country, which the otherwise pheno-
menally successful political and social framework of the
postwar years seems unable to deal with. Unemployment has
reached levels last seen during the Great Depression of the
early 1930s, and parts of the east are becoming depopulated
as their inhabitants move away in search of work. There are
fears that a declining and ageing population will be unable to
maintain the high standard of social welfare that Germans
have become used to. Bold action has become imperative for
future governments of whatever complexion.

Regional Diversity

For most of its history, Germany was not a united country,
but was divided into myriad states, their rulers a medley of
princes, dukes, margraves and bishops, as well as the occasional king. A number of prosperous cities proudly maintained
their independence. This has left an extraordinary array of
capital cities, some large, others quite small, but nearly all
with a heritage of palaces, gardens and art collections and, in
the case of the non-princely free towns, fine civic architecture.

Until 1871, Berlin was merely the capital of Prussia and,
despite its subsequent growing importance as the national
capital, other cities contin-
ued to think of themselves
as the natural focus of their
regions. This was especially
true in postwar West Ger-
many, with Berlin embedded
deep behind the Iron Curtain.

The largest of
Germany's *Länder*
is Bavaria (70,546 sq
km/27,238 sq miles),
the smallest the city
states of Hamburg
(755 sq km/292 sq miles)
and Bremen (404 sq
km/156 sq miles).

While the little Rhineland
town of Bonn became the
seat of the West German

government, cities such as Cologne, Düsseldorf, Frankfurt, Hanover and Hamburg flourished as near-metropolitan centres, with Frankfurt, for example, becoming the country's financial capital. Munich, seat of a monarch as recently as 1918, has never thought of itself as anything other than a capital city. The continuing importance of Germany's regions and regional capitals finds expression in the country's decentralised, federal political structure; its 16 states (*Land, Länder* plural) have many of the powers and responsibilities exercised in other countries by central government.

The parish church at Ramsau in the Bavarian Alps

Most of Germany's cities suffered terrible devastation in World War II. In the West, they were swiftly rebuilt, with many historic buildings immaculately restored. In the East, funds and sometimes the will were lacking for a comparable effort, but since reunification much has been accomplished; in 2005 Dresden's completely rebuilt Frauenkirche (Church of Our Lady) was finally reconsecrated.

Outside the cities, the countryside has a wealth of castles, palaces, abbeys and, in the Catholic south, pilgrimage churches. The countryside also forms a background to some of the most perfectly preserved small historic towns in Europe, foremost among them the succession of exquisite little cities like Rothenburg-ob-der-Tauber strung out along the Romantic Road heading southwards to the Alps.

Varied Landscapes

The most spectacular peaks are those of the Bavarian Alps, but mountains and upland massifs cover much of the country. Many of these areas are densely and beautifully wooded, providing endless opportunities for hiking or simply enjoying peace and quiet. Lakes abound, the largest, Lake Constance, is a veritable inland sea shared with Austria and Switzerland. Not so well known is the Mecklenburgische Seenplatte (Mecklenburg lake district), a glorious scattering of lakes of which the largest, the Müritzsee, is second only to Constance in extent. The upland massifs are threaded by rivers, the greatest of which is of course the Rhine, at its most scenic in the castle-studded gorge between Bingen and Koblenz. But

The chalk cliffs of the Nationalpark Jasmund on the island of Rügen

other waterways are just as attractive, especially where their banks are graced with vineyards, like the Mosel, Main and Neckar in the west, and the Saale and Elbe in the east. Quite different are the streams flowing through Brandenburg; widening into lake-like stretches and fringed with trees, they provide Berlin and its environs with a tranquil green setting.

One of Germany's best-kept holiday secrets, at least as far as visitors from abroad are concerned, is its coastline. The Germans themselves love the beaches of the North Sea and Baltic, less for their sun – though it does shine – than for the fresh air, the sea breezes, and the vast expanses of splendid sand. The German seaside is perhaps best enjoyed on one of the many islands, from Borkum, the westernmost of the Frisian islands, to Rügen in the Baltic, Germany's largest island, famous for its high cliffs of gleaming white chalk.

Green Germany

Woodlands cover something like a third of Germany's surface, a much-appreciated background to everyday life and the inspiration for much art and literature. Spruce, fir and pine dominate mountains and heathlands, and there are superb stands of beech, but the Germans' sacred tree is the stately oak, although Germany's oaks are suffering the effects of climate change, with one in every two oak trees officially sick. The feeling of the forest has been brought into town with great success; city parks are unequalled for quality and sheer extent, and there are street trees galore. Enthusiastic gardeners, Germans flock every two years to the *Bundesgartenschau*, the national garden festival. This is a moveable feast, held in different cities that use it to revamp existing parks or create new ones. Munich used the festival in 2005 to turn its old airport into superb parkland, while in 2007 and 2009 Gera and Schwerin will follow the example of other eastern cities to bring their green heritage up to scratch.

Green awareness works at all sorts of levels. Recycling waste is almost a national obsession, and the environmental impact of new developments such as motorways arouses fierce passions and often determined opposition. In the last decades of the 20th century, the ecologically minded Green Party increased its share of the vote; in 1998 it entered government in coalition with the Social Democrats. But in 2005 the party incurred losses, and along with more major losses for the SPD, the coalition no longer had a majority in the Bundestag.

Activities

As well as vibrant cities, fascinating small towns and inviting countryside, Germany has a generally well-off population with high expectations of how to spend its leisure time. As a result, there are plenty of recreational facilities, invariably designed to high standards and well maintained and run. They range from lavish theme parks to Olympic-sized swimming pools and well-signposted walking and cycling routes. The excellent roads and well-developed public transport make it easy to move around from one place to another. Dignified white steamers ply Lake Constance and the major rivers while silent electric craft skim the pristine waters of the Königsee, the least polluted of all the alpine lakes. Chairlifts and cable cars whisk sightseers to the tops of mountains, while all over the country, veteran steam trains chug along dozens of *Museumsbahnen*, preserved railway lines.

The majority of visitors from abroad come to Germany between May and September, when the weather is warm and occasionally too hot. July and August are the wettest months, though it is rare for rain to persist for more than a day or two; summer evenings can be quite cool. The big cities make excellent short-break destinations throughout the year. Winters bring cold, occasionally freezing weather, with fairly reliable snow cover in the Alps between December and March.

A BRIEF HISTORY

Even more than most great European countries, Germany has had a turbulent history. The nation had to wait until the late 19th century to achieve unity, only to lose it after defeat in World War II. Greeted initially with great joy, the reunification of 1990 has not been an unqualified success, and has reminded many Germans that most of their history has been a story of division and conflict as well as striking achievement in many spheres.

Germans and Romans

In the final centuries BC, much of the area of present-day Germany was occupied by Celtic peoples. By the time the Roman Empire began its northward expansion in the 1st century BC, the Celts had moved away, escaping the pressure of Germanic tribes leaving their ancestral lands to the north and east. After their conquest of Celtic Gaul – today's France – the Romans turned eastwards, pushing the empire's frontier to the line of the Rhine and Danube. First contact with the Germans lurking in their vast forests inclined the Romans to dismiss them as indolent barbar-

Hermann, conqueror of legions and the first Germanic hero

ians, given to excessive eating and drinking, and quarrelling violently among themselves. Attempts to bring them within the orbit of the empire included inviting prominent tribesmen to be educated in Rome and serve in the Roman army. This policy backfired when one German so privileged returned to his roots, roused his people to resist Roman expansion and, at the Battle of the Teutoburger Wald in AD9, roundly defeated the legionary army sent to punish him. This first Germanic hero was Hermann, whose resistance to Rome gave him cult-like status to German nationalists of a much later date.

Following their defeat, the Romans prudently remained on the Rhine, giving the lands to the west of the river their usual treatment of ruler-straight roads, well-planned towns and luxurious villas. They also introduced Christianity and the cultivation of the vine. Even today, many feel that the Romanised Rhineland remains distinct from the rest of Germany.

Charlemagne

The collapse of the Roman Empire in the 4th century AD was in part brought about by the restlessness of the Germanic tribes, who refused to be confined to their homelands. Langobards moved south to Italy, where Lombardy is called after them, while Vandals marauded through Spain into North Africa, giving their name to a particular kind of destructive behaviour. The most powerful group was the Franks, whose realm extended east and west of present-day Belgium. Their greatest ruler was Charles the Great (Charlemagne in French), Karl der Grosse in German, who forced the submission of the Saxons and other German dukedoms and created a cen-

> The memory of the Franks is preserved in names like France (Frankreich in German), Frankfurt, where they forded the River Main, and the province of Franconia (Franken).

tralised feudal state. He deliberately associated himself with the glory and prestige of Roman rule, having himself crowned emperor by Pope Leo III in Rome in the year 800. Though his main base was at Aachen, Charles constantly moved around his dominions from one Imperial palace to the next, setting a pattern for later emperors and putting off the emergence of a geographical centre and capital city for Germany as a whole.

Emperors, Princes and Popes

Later rulers of what came to be known as the 'Holy Roman Empire of the German Nation' failed to exercise the same measure of control as Charlemagne. Throughout the Middle Ages, nominally subordinate princes and other petty rulers repeatedly contested the authority of the emperor, the focus of whose attention was frequently on his possessions in Italy and on his relations with the pope. From the Vatican, successive

A pope and an emperor depicted in stained glass, Cologne Cathedral

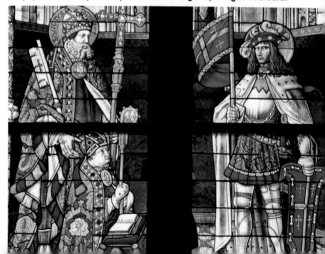

popes interfered in German affairs, asserting their supremacy as spiritual ruler over that of the emperor as temporal lord, and undermining him by encouraging his underlings to rebel. Though Germany thus remained divided, there was much progress. Led by Lübeck, the Hanseatic League of trading cities promoted commerce along the shores of the Baltic and beyond; great cities like Nuremberg began their rise, and German settlers colonised much of Slavonic central and eastern Europe, founding towns and villages and bringing Christianity with them, sometimes at the point of the sword. In the middle of the 15th century, Johann Gutenberg of Mainz ushered in a new era with his invention of moveable type, revolutionising book production.

Martin Luther

Reformation and War

Gutenberg's invention helped spread criticism of a Church that had become lazy and corrupt, and ensured that the teachings of reformer Martin Luther (1483–1546) reached a wide audience. Luther's ideas were taken up by many German rulers, one of whom, Friedrich III of Saxony, gave him sanctuary in Wartburg Castle. By the mid 16th century, Germany's division into a complex patchwork of Protestant and Catholic domains was complete, with Lutheranism dominating the north, Catholicism the south. Far from bringing stability, this arrangement led to the horrors of the Thirty Years' War (1618–48), in which German fought German, foreign powers like France and Sweden sought their own advantage, and mercenary soldiers plundered and pillaged at will. The war only came to an end with the total exhaustion of the combatants, leaving a devastated and depopulated landscape.

French Dominance

In the aftermath of war, France became the leading power in Europe, and it was France that German rulers admired and sought to imitate. The Holy Roman Empire was a much diminished force; the office of emperor was now permanently filled by a member of the Habsburg Dynasty, who, from his seat in Vienna was less interested in German affairs than in the opportunities offered by the gradual Turkish retreat from Hungary and the Balkans. All over Germany, princes strove to turn their residences into a facsimile of Louis XIV's glittering court at Versailles. Palaces were extravagantly built or rebuilt in baroque style and provided with formal gardens on the French model, while in the court French was spoken, and the great prize was to have some French savant in residence, like Voltaire at Frederick the Great's Schloss Sanssouci at Potsdam. High culture flourished in this era, though not necessarily under the patronage of princes; at Leipzig, it was the city council that employed Johann Sebastian Bach as town musician and choirmaster.

As the 18th century progressed, it became clear that Prussia was the coming power. Prussian monarchs ruled their realm on rational lines, promoting agriculture and industry, dispensing justice firmly but fairly, and creating a well-disciplined standing army capable of realising their territorial ambitions. But as the century ended, and the flames of the French Revolution spread all over Europe, no German power proved capable of stemming the conflagration.

Napoleon and the Rise of Nationalism

For the first decade of the 19th century, it was a Frenchman, Napoleon Bonaparte, who determined the fate of Germany; he turned Bavaria, Württemberg and Saxony into kingdoms, amalgamated other German states into a subservient 'Confederation of the Rhine', and finally abolished the moribund Holy Roman Empire.

Napoleon's retreat from Moscow in 1812 unleashed passionate opposition to French domination as well as patriotic hopes for a new era of German unity and democracy. In 1813, Napoleon's army was bloodily defeated at Leipzig, at what came to be called the Battle of the Nations. But at the Congress of Vienna in 1815 the old order was restored, albeit tidied up, with dozens of minor German states abolished and absorbed into a new grouping of 39 sovereign units including a much-enlarged Prussia. For nearly 50 years, reactionary rulers succeeded in keeping the lid on subversive aspirations; an attempted revolution in 1848 petered out when the would-be revolutionaries argued interminably at their parliament in Frankfurt about the boundaries of a united Germany and how it should be ruled. But the genie of nationalism was now firmly out of the bottle, and it was only to be a matter of time before the country's unification was achieved.

The Second Reich

In the end, German unity was brought about, not by upheaval from below or by reasoned discussion, but by cynical diplomacy and armed force, under the leadership of an increasingly militaristic Prussia. A brief and victorious war with Austria in 1866 excluded the Habsburgs from German affairs, and left Prussia free to mould Germany as she wished. This she was able to do thanks to the skill and ruthlessness of her chancellor, Otto von Bismarck, who engineered another war, this time with France. Most of the other German states rallied to Prussia's side and victory was soon achieved. German unity was proclaimed in the Palace of Versailles in 1871, with Wilhelm I of Prussia as German emperor. Successor to the First Reich – the Holy Roman Empire – the Second Reich prospered and soon challenged the pre-eminence of Britain and France, particularly after the foolhardy and unstable Kaiser Wilhelm II succeeded to the throne in 1888.

Otto von Bismarck

World War I

By the early 20th century Germany was a contradictory mixture: a great industrial power with a skilled and educated workforce, trade unions and advanced social legislation, but ruled by a monarch and court clad in medieval trappings and engaged in a game of international brinkmanship. When Austrian Archduke Franz Ferdinand was shot by a Serb assassin at Sarajevo in June 1914, Germany recklessly encouraged Austria to declare war on Serbia. Europe's interlocking alliances were activated, with the 'central powers' of Austria and Germany facing Russia and France. Britain was drawn in when Germany violated Belgian neutrality, part of a long-prepared war plan to eliminate France quickly before turning on Russia. The plan failed when the German armies were stopped just short of Paris. Germany could not hope to win the war of attrition that followed, least of all when the United States entered the struggle in 1917, provoked by German submarine attacks on her shipping. By late 1918 defeat loomed, though the generals managed to deflect blame for it on to a newly formed republican government, thereby creating the toxic legend of an unvanquished army betrayed by a civilian 'stab in the back'. Wilhelm II went into ignominious exile in the Netherlands.

Weimar

In the chaotic situation following the armistice, the new government fled from revolutionary disturbances in Berlin to the safety of the small provincial town of Weimar. The little city gave its name to the democratic republic which somehow survived multiple misfortunes: the loss of territory to France and Poland, onerous reparation payments to the Allies, attempts to topple it from Right and Left, a French occupation of the Ruhr industrial area, and catastrophic inflation which destroyed the savings of the middle classes. By the late 1920s a degree of prosperity had returned, social reforms were in place, and it seemed as if liberal democracy might have a future. But the Great Depression of 1929 intervened; by 1932

Weimar Culture

The Weimar years saw a flowering of cultural creativity. Literature and music flourished, and the sharpest of satirical cabarets enlivened the Berlin scene. German artists, designers and architects led the world, with the Bauhaus design school in Dessau becoming a byword for Modernist innovation. When the Nazis clamped down on such activity, the exiled professors and practitioners continued their work elsewhere, notably in the United States, where luminaries like Mies van der Rohe and Walter Gropius helped lay the foundations of a truly contemporary architecture.

German industry had collapsed, there were six million unemployed, and Nazis and Communists were confidently offering rival totalitarian solutions to the country's problems, as well as brawling with each other for control of the streets. Fearing a Red Revolution, in January 1933 the German establishment appointed Nazi Party leader Adolf Hitler as chancellor.

Nazi torchlit parade, 1933

The Third Reich

Hitler moved swiftly to consolidate his power, using the burning-down of the Reichstag in February 1933 as a pretext for imprisoning and intimidating his opponents and subsequently ruling by decree. An ambitious programme of re-armament and public works helped defeat unemployment, while a string of foreign-policy triumphs, such as the annexation of Austria, overcame the humiliations suffered in 1918. The Nazis brought latent anti-Semitism into play, with the Jews made the scapegoat for all Germany's ills and forced into ever more constricting circumstances. Those who realised what was coming, emigrated, along with a sizeable proportion of the country's cultural elite. Popular enthusiasm was maintained by means of stunning spectacles such as the Berlin Olympics of 1936 and the annual Nuremberg rallies. The young were conscripted into the Hitler Youth and turned into the regime's most fanatical supporters.

To many it seemed as if the frustrated nationalism of the 19th century had finally borne fruit.

World War II

Despite widespread support for the Nazi regime, many Germans were dismayed when war broke out in September 1939. A series of swift victories won by *Blitzkrieg* tactics over Poland, the Low Countries and France followed. However, the failure to eliminate Britain in the summer of 1940, the attack on the Soviet Union in June 1941 and the entry of the USA into the war in December of that year faced Germany with a coalition whose overwhelming superiority in resources meant that they must ultimately prevail. But Hitler could only conceive of death and destruction, and many of his minions in the SS were more interested in implementing the Final Solution – the murder of Europe's Jews – than winning the war. Two events sealed Germany's fate: the 1943 defeat at Stalingrad in the east, and the 1944 Normandy invasion in the west. In July 1944, an attempted assassination of Hitler by a group of army officers failed. The war went on for almost another year, causing more carnage and destruction than in the previous five put together. By April 1945 Hitler was dead, Germany's cities had been bombed into ruins, and millions of Germans had abandoned their homelands in the east for fear of a vengeful Red Army.

Allied bombs reduced many cities to rubble

Germany Divided

The victorious Allied forces now occupied Germany. After a short period of uneasy postwar cooperation between the western powers and the Soviets, each side created rival Germanys in its own image. In the west, the Bundesrepublik Deutschland, or Federal Republic of Germany, had a liberal democratic constitution and a burgeoning economy. In the east was the Deutsche Demokratische Republik (DDR), or German Democratic Republic (GDR), a 'people's democracy' run on the lines of the Soviet Union's other satellites in Eastern Europe, and lagging well behind the West in economic achievement. Embedded in the GDR was Berlin, likewise divided into an eastern and western sector, the latter only having survived a year-long Soviet blockade in 1948–9 thanks to the near-miracle of the Berlin Airlift, in which US and British planes flew in every necessity of life, including bulk loads such as coal.

West Berlin proved a thorn in the GDR's side, allowing its dissatisfied citizens easy escape to the West. By 1961, some three million had left, and the collapse of the economy was only averted by building the Berlin Wall to keep the population in. Over the next three decades the GDR portrayed itself as one of the success stories of Communism. Statistics were manipulated to show that it was one of the world's leading industrial powers, with a welfare system that cared for its citizens from cradle to grave. In reality, the goods being produced were only saleable in Eastern Europe, polluting industries were destroying the environment, and social welfare existed alongside the *Stasi*, a secret police apparatus of almost unimaginable scope and complexity. By the late 1980s, the system was foundering; in 1989 popular discontent manifested itself in huge street demonstrations, and the regime's collapse became inevitable when Mikail Gorbachev's Soviet Union withdrew its support.

Die Wende

Meaning 'the turning point', 'die Wende' is the German term for the momentous changes that took place following the collapse of the Berlin Wall on 9 November 1989. For a while, it seemed possible that an East German state of some kind might continue to exist, even after the Communist regime had realised that the game was up and had handed over power to an interim government. Many felt that the differences between the two German states were so profound that a period of transition would be needed before any decision about reunification could be taken. But the West German Chancellor, Helmut Kohl, had no such doubts; greeted by enthusiastic crowds on his tours of the East, he declared 'My goal… is the unity of the nation!' At the elections held in March 1990, the eastern branch of his Christian Democrat Party secured an overwhelming victory, clearing the way for swift reunification. To great public rejoicing this duly took place on 9 October, not as some new confederation, but as a straightforward absorption of the GDR into the Bundesrepublik. Chancellor Kohl promised his new citizens 'blossoming landscapes', but despite huge investment in the

At the heart of the EU

East this shared prosperity and wellbeing is taking far longer to achieve than Kohl and his listeners ever imagined. Despite this, and an unemployment figure hovering between four and five million in the first years of the 21st century, Germany's industrial might has not diminished; the country now tops the world rankings for the export of goods.

Historical Landmarks

5th-1st century BC Germany inhabited by Celts.

58BC Julius Caesar halts westwards move by Germanic tribes.

9AD Romans defeated at the Battle of the Teutoburger Wald.

4th–5th centuries Collapse of the Roman Empire; westwards migration of Germanic peoples.

6th century Emergence of the Frankish kingdom.

800 Frankish ruler Charlemagne crowned Holy Roman Emperor.

1241 Foundation of Hanseatic League of ports and trading cities.

1386 Foundation of the first German university, at Heidelberg.

c1450 Invention of moveable type by Johann Gutenberg.

1517 Luther nails his 95 theses to the church door at Wittenberg, marking the start of the Reformation.

1618–48 Thirty Years' War devastates and depopulates Central Europe.

1701 Rise of Prussia begins with crowning of Elector Friedrich III as king.

1806 Napoleon dominates Germany with the creation of the Confederation of the Rhine and the abolition of the Holy Roman Empire.

1813 Napoleon's defeat at the 'Battle of the Nations'.

1815 Congress of Vienna disappoints hopes for German unity.

1848–49 Failure of attempted revolution.

1871 Prussian King Wilhelm proclaimed emperor of united Germany.

1914–18 World War I ends in defeat of Germany and foundation of Weimar Republic.

1923 Hyperinflation; occupation of the Ruhr by France.

1933 Nazi Party leader Adolf Hitler appointed Reich chancellor.

1945 Defeat of Nazi Germany ends World War II in Europe.

1949 Division into western Federal Republic and Communist-led German Democratic Republic.

1961 Berlin Wall built to stem GDR's loss of population to West Germany.

1989 Berlin Wall demolished; collapse of Communist regime.

1990 GDR absorbed into the Federal Republic; Germany reunited.

2005 Angela Merkel, leader of the conservative Christian Democrats (CDU), becomes Germany's first female chancellor.

WHERE TO GO

BERLIN AND POTSDAM

Still in the throes of reinventing itself as the capital of a reunited Germany, Berlin is one of the most dynamic and exciting cities of Europe, attracting enthusiastic visitors in their tens of thousands from around the globe. The city's most potent symbol, the Brandenburger Tor (Brandenburg Gate), now stands at its heart, rather than marking the division between East and West as it once did.

Nearby, the restored Reichstag once more houses the nation's parliament, while the Mitte district, the historic city centre, has emerged from Communist drabness, its museums, galleries, theatres and other monuments forming one of the world's great cultural ensembles. The artery of Friedrichstrasse is once more lined with prestigious retail palaces and glittering shopping arcades, their equivalents in western Berlin the well-established stores lining the boulevard of Kurfürstendamm. New life has been breathed into inner-city boroughs like Prenzlauer Berg, with its cafés, restaurants and nightlife, while Kreuzberg remains the stronghold of alternative lifestyles and of Berlin's Turkish population. To the west, affluent suburban boroughs like Wilmersdorf and Zehlendorf benefit from the vast city forest of the Grunewald and the chain of lakes along the River Havel.

Berlin generally is a wonderfully green city, with a heritage of parks and open spaces only equalled by those of Potsdam, the regal little city just to the west where princes, kings and emperors built their palaces in a glorious setting. Potsdam is the capital of the *Land* of Brandenburg, a quiet countryside of sandy soils, pine forests and slow-moving rivers.

Potsdamer Platz

Brandenburger Tor

Brandenburg Gate Area

Marking the western boundary of the city when it was built in 1791, the **Brandenburger Tor** is Berlin's last remaining gateway. The scene of many a military parade in past times, the gate is now best remembered as the backdrop to the ecstatic scenes which took place following the fall of the Berlin Wall. The famous Quadriga, a statue of Victory driving her four-horse chariot, is a replica, the original having been destroyed in World War II.

To the east and west stretch broad, straight thoroughfares. Leading to Museum Island, the boulevard of **Unter den Linden** ('Beneath the Lime Trees') was laid out by Prussian rulers as

> The design of the Brandenburg Gate was inspired by the Propylea, the grand entrance to the Acropolis in Athens, and was originally called the Friedenstor (Gate of Peace).

their most prestigious street and lined with dignified neo-classical buildings. Facing each other are the State Opera and Humboldt University, while in the grid of streets to the south is the **Gendarmenmarkt**, a glorious architectural ensemble of buildings including French and German cathedrals.

On the far side of the Brandenburger Tor, the Strasse des 17 Juni (17 June Street) penetrates the **Tiergarten**, the vast and splendid parkland which was once a royal hunting preserve. The Tiergarten is a wonderful asset to have in the centre of a metropolis, though its trees are almost all relatively recent plantings, most of their predecessors having been felled for fuel in the difficult postwar period. It makes a leafy setting for various structures, among them the Soviet War Memorial.

To the north is the new government quarter, its cool, modern buildings spanning the River Spree and symbolically breaking down the old boundary between East and West Berlin. One focal point here is the box-like Kanzleramt, the office of the federal chancellor, but anchoring today's government to the country's past is the massive **Reichstag** (open 8am–midnight, last admission 10pm; free). Completed in 1894, in 1933 the Reichstag was gutted by a fire almost certainly started by the Nazis, and further devastated by Allied bombing and by the fierce fighting of April–May 1945. Since 1999 it has once more been the seat of parliament, its forbidding exterior lightened by the superb glass and steel cupola placed atop it by the British architect Sir Norman Foster and illuminating the debating chamber with natural light.

The cupola of the Reichstag

Museum Island

Enclosed between two arms of the River Spree, Berlin's **Museumsinsel** (Museum Island) formed part of the original, 13th-century core of the city. It owes its name to the cluster of world-class museums which contain some of the country's finest collections. The island is reached from Unter den Linden via the elegant **Schlossbrücke**, designed by the great Prussian architect Karl Friedrich Schinkel in 1824. On the northern side of the approach to the bridge is the baroque **Zeughaus** (Arsenal) – the home of the **Deutsches Historisches Museum** (German Historical Museum; open daily 10am–6pm; admission fee) – and, next door, the **Neue Wache** (New Guardhouse), a perfectly proportioned little neo-Grecian temple by Schinkel now dedicated to the victims of war and tyranny.

Beyond the bridge is Schinkel's masterpiece, the neo-classical **Altes Museum** (open Tues–Sun 10am–6pm; admission fee), its long colonnaded façade overlooking the grassy expanse of the Lustgarten. It houses an outstanding collection of classical antiquities.

To its rear is the **Alte Nationalgalerie** (open Tues–Sun 10am–6pm, Thur until 10pm; admission fee), which houses an excellent collection of 19th-century German art. Still undergoing restoration, the **Neues Museum** will eventually house the pre- and early history collections, including superlative items from ancient Egypt like the famous bust of Nefertiti.

Pergamon treasures

The most grandiose of the island's museums is the **Pergamonmuseum** (open

Tues–Sun 10am–6pm, Thur until 10pm; admission fee), named after its most prized possession, the gigantic marble altar from the Hellenistic city of Pergamon, in Turkey. But this is just one of countless treasures from the world of classical antiquity, the Middle East and the Orient; make sure you see the great gateway from the Roman town of Miletus and the famous Ishtar Gate from Babylon. At the very tip of Museum Island, the **Bodemuseum** is scheduled to reopen in 2006 as a permanent home for a range of collections including the half-million items

Berliner Dom and the River Spree

of the world-famous Münzkabinett (coin collecton).

The Lustgarten is dominated by the formidable bulk of the **Berliner Dom** (open Mon–Sat 9am–8pm, Sun noon–7pm; admission fee), the cathedral completed in 1905 as the court church of the Hohenzollern royal family. Its bombastic architecture perfectly evokes the spirit of Kaiser Wilhelm II's time. Official architecture of a very different era can be seen opposite; the bronzed glass and steel **Palast der Republik** (Palace of the Republic) was built in 1976 as the seat of the GDR parliament on the site of the demolished Prussian Stadtschloss (City Palace). Closed in 1990, and sadly decayed, the asbestos-ridden edifice awaits demolition, enabling the Stadtschloss to be rebuilt.

Checkpoint Charlie

Towards the southern end of Friedrichstrasse, this most notorious crossing-point between East and West has become one of Berlin's most popular sights. It was here, shortly after the building of the Berlin Wall in 1961, that US and Soviet tanks faced each other in one of the most tense stand-offs of the

---

Remembering Hitler's Victims

Berlin, which had harboured an exceptionally large and vibrant Jewish community, will never be forgotten as the place from which the extermination of European Jewry was planned and directed. In May 2005, 60 years after the end of World War II, the **Memorial to the Murdered Jews of Europe** was opened in the presence of Holocaust survivors. Spreading over an extensive area to the south of the Brandenburg Gate, and designed by the American architect Peter Eisenmann, it consists of a vast and enigmatic field of 2,711 concrete slabs. Another American, Polish-born Daniel Libeskind, was responsible for what has become one of Berlin's most visited museums, the **Jüdisches Museum** (Jewish Museum; open Mon 10am–10pm, Tues–Sun 10am–8pm; admission fee), its jagged outline and disorientating interior evocative of the troubled course of German-Jewish history.

The decision to proceed to the 'Final Solution' was taken in the deceptively idyllic lakeside surroundings of the Wannsee, where the **Haus der Wannsee-Konferenz** (open Mon–Fri 10am–6pm, Sat–Sun 2–6pm; free) preserves chilling mementoes of the fateful meeting of 20 January 1941 presided over by Reinhard Heydrich and attended by Adolf Eichmann.

German resistance to the Nazi regime is commemorated in the **Gedenkstätte Deutscher Widerstand** (open Mon–Fri 9am–6pm, Thur until 8pm, Sat–Sun 10am–6pm; free). Located in the former Wehrmacht (Army) HQ, this is where Count Stauffenberg and other officers who had attempted to assassinate Hitler were summarily executed.

Cold War. Visitors are invited to pose with menacing-looking members of the People's Police or take a trip in a Trabant, the once-ubiquitous East German 'people's car'. But perhaps more rewarding is the **Haus am Checkpoint Charlie – Mauermuseum** (Checkpoint Charlie Building – Berlin Wall Museum; open daily 9am–10pm; admission fee), whose displays feature the attempts made by East Germans to overcome the barrier of the Berlin Wall. Home-made aircraft and submarines were among the often ingenious means of escape.

Alexanderplatz and Around

The draughty expanses on either side of the elevated Alexanderplatz railway station were the showcase of East Berlin in Communist times. Soaring over it all is the 365-m (1,198-ft) **Fernsehturm** (TV Tower; viewing gallery open daily 9am–1am; admission fee), deliberately designed to upstage West Berlin's far more modest Funkturm (Radio Tower). The panorama from the top takes in the whole of the city, and there is a revolving restaurant. Among the few remaining historic structures at the foot of the tower are the 13th-century brick-built **Marienkirche** and the 19th-century **Rotes Rathaus** (Red Town Hall), also built of brick though in a very different architectural style. Beyond the railway overpass, the high-rise slab of the Park Inn (formerly the 'Stadt Berlin', the GDR's foremost hotel) looks down on the rather tacky Weltzeituhr (World Time Clock) and the Brunnen der Völkerfreundschaft (Fountain of Friendship between the Peoples).

Rotes Rathaus and the Fernsehturm

Leading eastwards is the broad boulevard of Karl-Marx-Allee, laid out in the 1950s and known at the time as Stalin-Allee. The Soviet-inspired architecture of the apartment buildings lining it is now appreciated as a historic style in its own right, and many of the blocks have been restored.

More obviously appealing is the architecture of the **Niko-laiviertel** to the south of the Rotes Rathaus. Centred on the twin-steepled Nikolaikirche, this little neighbourhood was completely rebuilt in near-authentic historic style as part of the city's 750th anniversary celebrations in 1987, and its intimate atmosphere, cafés, restaurants and shops have proved a great hit with visitors to the city.

Equally popular but with a different atmosphere altogether is the thriving area around **Hackescher Markt**, one S-Bahn stop west of Alexanderplatz. Very run-down in GDR times, this district is now buzzing with bars, cafés, clubs, galleries, art workshops, antiques dealers and independent shops. The area's centrepiece is the immaculately restored **Hackesche Höfe**, an Art Deco complex of interconnecting courtyards and buildings. Oranienburger Strasse leads from here to one of the great monuments of Jewish Berlin, the splendid **Neue Syna-goge** (open Sun–Thur 10am–6pm, Fri 10am–2pm; admission fee), its gleaming cupola visible from far away.

Kurfürstendamm and Around

One of the great landmarks of West Berlin is the ruined **Kaiser-Wilhelm-Gedächtnis-Kirche** (Kaiser Wilhelm Memorial Church), its bomb-blasted tower preserved as an instantly recognisable landmark and known to wise-cracking Berliners as the 'hollow tooth'. Flanked by a modern church and belltower, it stands on Bretscheidplatz, one of the city's favourite meeting places.

To the north is the **Zoologischer Garten** (Zoo; open daily 9am–6.30pm with seasonal variations; admission fee), which has one of the richest and most varied animal collections in Europe. The nearby mainline railway and S-Bahn station and bus terminus is Berlin's busiest transport hub.

To the southeast, along Tauentzienstrasse, stands one of the world's great department stores, KaDeWe (Kaufhaus des Westens), a tourist attraction in its own right, not least because of its lavish sixth-floor delicatessen. Further tempting retail opportunities multiply as you head west along Berlin's great shopping artery, **Kurfürstendamm**, known simply as Ku'damm. Perhaps less glamorous now than in its 1950s and 60s heyday, its broad pavements still invite you to stroll and window-shop.

There are more fascinating shops, boutiques, cafés and restaurants in the streets and squares to the north, particularly around Savignyplatz. Before leaving Ku'damm you might like to visit the Story of Berlin (open daily 10am–6pm; admission fee), which has excellent multimedia displays tracing the city's turbulent past.

Kulturforum and Potsdamer Platz

Developed by West Berlin at a time when the city's division seemed permanent, the Kulturforum cultural complex rivals Museum Island in quality, though its collections are of a very different nature. The first building on

Berlin **sculpture, with the Memorial Church**

the site, in 1963, was the tent-like structure of the **Philhar-monie**, designed by Hans Scharoun, its form perfectly reflecting its function as a superlative concert hall. Scharoun also built the adjoining **Musikinstrumenten-Museum** (open Tues–Fri 9am–5pm, Thur until 10pm, Sat–Sun 10am–5pm; admission fee), which has a fine collection of historic instruments, among them a Stradivarius violin of 1703 and an Art Deco Wurlitzer organ.

On the far side of the street, a sprawling structure houses several galleries. Foremost among them is the **Gemälde-galerie** (Picture Gallery; open Tues–Fri 10am–6pm, Thur 10am–10pm, Sat–Sun 10am–6pm; admission fee), home of some of the world's finest paintings. Works by virtually all the great names in European art from the 13th to the 18th century can be found here; German Old Masters like Dürer and Cranach are particularly strongly represented and the Rembrandt collection is exceptional.

Also in this part of the Kulturforum are two smaller museums. The **Kupferstichkabinett** (Museum of Prints and Drawings; open Tues–Fri 10am–6pm, Sat–Sun 11am–6pm; admission fee) encompasses graphic art from the Middle Ages to the present. The **Kunstgewerbemuseum** (Museum of Decorative Arts; open Tues–Fri 10am-6pm, Sat–Sun 11am–6pm; admission fee) has a magnificent collection of European arts and crafts and interior design, from medieval and Renaissance hand-made treasures to examples of contemporary industrial output.

Standing out among the late 20th-century buildings of the Kulturforum is the delicately detailed 19th-century neo-Romanesque brick church of St Matthew. It contrasts strikingly with the uncompromisingly modern **Neue Nationalgalerie** (New National Gallery; open Tues–Fri 10am–6pm, Thur 10am–10pm, Sat–Sun 11am–6pm; admission fee), a steel and glass building by Mies van der Rohe. As well as staging

The Neue Nationalgalerie

changing exhibitions of contemporary art, the gallery houses one of the country's finest collections of works by 20th-century German artists and their international counterparts.

On the far bank of the Landwehr Canal is the extensive and fascinating **Deutsches Technikmuseum** (German Technology Museum; open Tues–Fri 9am–5.30pm, Sat–Sun 10am–6pm; admission fee). Poised above its entrance is a DC3 aircraft that took part in the Berlin Airlift. Inside, full-size exhibits and interactive displays deal with every aspect of technology from trains to textiles.

To the east of the Kulturforum, the entertainment, shopping and business centre of **Potsdamer Platz** has become one of the great symbols of post-unification Berlin. Its striking contemporary structures include the **Sony Centre**, whose stunning transparent dome shelters a spacious piazza. Here too is the **Film Museum Berlin** (open Tues–Sun 10am–6pm, Thur 10am–8pm; admission fee), which celebrates the glory days of Berlin as Germany's Hollywood and includes a great deal of Marlene Dietrich memorabilia.

Charlottenburg and Far Western Berlin

One of the best places to experience the atmosphere of Prussian Berlin is the glorious rococo and baroque palace of **Schloss Charlottenburg** (open Tues–Fri 9am–5pm, Sat–Sun 10am–5pm; admission fee). Painstakingly restored after wartime damage, the interiors are of great sumptuousness, and are complemented by the park bounded by the winding River Spree. Further to the west stands the **Olympiastadion** (open daily 10am–4pm, possibly later; may be closed for events; admission fee), its huge scale and mock classical architecture redolent of the Third Reich; it was built for the 1936 Nazi Olympics and was comprehensively refurbished for the 2006 football World Cup.

The Dahlem district is home to the **Museumsquartier Dahlem**, another of the city's museum complexes. There are lavishly stocked museums of East Asian art and Indian art and others dealing with enthnography and European folk art

---

Berliner Schnauze

Like big-city folk in most countries, Berliners are renowned for their sharp wit and an unforgiving view of the world and its ways, sometimes described as *Berliner Schnauze* (Berlin lip). Pretentiousness is quickly deflated, notably in the nicknames given to certain features of the city. Thus the gaunt ruin of the Kaiser-Wilhelm Church became the 'Hollow Tooth', the bulbous Congress Hall the 'Pregnant Oyster', and the East Berlin TV Tower the 'Pope's Revenge' because of the big cross formed on its reflective surface by the sun. More recently, the federal chancellor's office, a big white boxy structure, has become known as the 'washing machine'.

(all museums open Tues–Fri 10am–6pm, Sat–Sun 11am–6pm; admission fee).

To the west of Dahlem and the other leafy suburbs extends the **Grunewald** forest, vast enough to get lost in and still the haunt of wild boar.

Beyond the trees, the glorious waters of the Wannsee, a linked pair of lakes on the River Havel, form one of Berlin's favourite recreation spots, its beaches crowded with swimmers and sun-worshippers in warm weath-

Sculpture at Charlottenburg

er. There's a foretaste here of the splendours of royal Potsdam, with palaces and lovely parklands on Pfaueninsel (Peacock Island) and at Volkspark Klein-Glienicke. A pretty little temple at Klein-Glienicke overlooks the Glienicke bridge, famous as the East–West crossing point where Cold War rivals occasionally swapped spies in a tense atmosphere of mutual suspicion.

Potsdam

The capital of the *Land* of Brandenburg, **Potsdam**, about 30km (19 miles) southwest of the capital, is to Berlin what Versailles is to Paris, a royal residential town set among woods and lakeland, embellished with fine architecture and lovely man-made landscapes. Most of the rulers of Prussia left their mark here, most notably Frederick the Great, builder of Potsdam's outstanding palace, Sanssouci.

The centre of the little city was devastated in an Allied air raid in the final days of World War II, and suffered further neglect and demolition under the Communist regime. But

Schloss Sanssouci

there's still plenty to see, from the massive early 19th-century domed **Nikolaikirche** to the gracious streets and villa quarters once occupied by Prussian officials and the officers of the city's important garrison. The charming, brick-built **Holländisches Viertel** (Dutch Quarter), laid out in the mid-18th century for immigrants from the Netherlands, now acts as a magnet for locals and visitors alike, with an inviting range of bars, restaurants and boutiques.

Beyond Potsdam's own Brandenburg Gate at the western end of the town centre stretches the parkland of **Schloss Sanssouci** (palace open Tues–Sun 9am–5pm, until 4pm in winter; admission fee). The park is the leafy framework for an array of statuary, fountains, temples, residences and pavilions, the most exquisite of which is the **Chinesisches Teehaus** (Chinese Teahouse; open Tues–Sun 10am–5pm), which contains a collection of fine porcelain. And then there are the palaces. A flight of terraces intended for the cultivation of fruit and vines leads to the palace of Sanssouci, which was designed by Frederick the Great's architect Georg Wenzeslaus von Knobelsdorff and completed in 1747. Its elegant interiors were the scene of much music-making, philosophising and high-minded conversation, for Frederick prided himself on his culture, even managing to attract French philosopher Voltaire to be an ornament of his court. At the far end of the park stands a very different sort of palace, the **Neues Palais**, also built by Frederick but of overpowering size and ostentation.

In 1945, Schloss Cecilienhof was the venue for a meeting at which the Allied heads of government – Stalin, Churchill and Truman – settled the division of Europe after World War II.

In complete contrast, on the other side of the city is **Schloss Cecilienhof** (open daily 9am–5pm; admission fee), an imitation Tudor country house only completed during World War I for Kaiser Wilhelm's son, the crown prince. It is now a luxury hotel.

Spreewald

Between Berlin and the border town of Cottbus, the River Spree spreads out into a kind of inland delta, its countless channels shaded by overhanging trees. This is the tranquil Spreewald, one of the homelands of the Sorbs, the country's tiny Slav minority, whose ancestors retreated here and thus managed to resist Germanisation. There's an open-air museum of their traditional buildings at **Lehde** (open daily 10am–6pm), close to the area's little capital of **Lübbenau**. Movement in this trackless wilderness was traditionally by punt, craft still used to ferry the visitors around who come here in their thousands to escape the pressures of the city. But it's easy to avoid the crowds, by walking, cycling or taking to the water in a hired canoe.

Hamburg and its waterfront

HAMBURG AND THE NORTH

Between the Dutch, Danish and Polish borders are some of Germany's most fascinating cities, many of them standing at the point where great rivers flow into the North Sea or the Baltic. Foremost among them are the city states of Hamburg and Bremen, followed closely by other harbour towns which were once proud members of the Hanseatic League, the all-powerful trading association, and which have preserved much of their heritage.

The coast itself is almost infinitely varied, with islands, glorious sandy beaches, rich wildlife, dune systems, steep bluffs, wooded tracts and chalk cliffs. Busy seaside towns alternate with tranquil islands where traffic is banned, while the Baltic shore is graced by resorts little changed since their heyday a century ago. Inland is the extensive Mecklenburgische Seenplatte (Mecklenburg lake district), with its many lakes and deep forests.

➤ Hamburg

More than 100km (60 miles) upstream from the mouth of the mighty River Elbe, Germany's second city is its largest port, its media capital and an important manufacturing centre. It's also a place of great contrasts; it boasts more millionaires than anywhere else in the country, but unemployment is high, and its generally sober ethos sits awkwardly with the raucous lifestyle epitomised by the city's red-light district, the Reeperbahn.

Hamburg began life as Hammaburg, a 9th-century fortress built by Charlemagne at the confluence of the little River Alster and the Elbe. For centuries the city lived in the shadow of Lübeck, the leader of the Hanseatic League, but once trading patterns had shifted from the Baltic to the wider world of the Atlantic, Hamburg never looked back. This despite having to rebuild itself from scratch twice, once after a terrible blaze in 1842, and again after the devastating firestorm unleashed 101 years later by the Royal Air Force. Created a Free Imperial city in 1618, Hamburg considers itself a cut above the rest of Germany, a status confirmed by its continued existence as a *Land* in its own right. And its cultural life and its heritage of museums are the equal of many a capital city.

> **Less dramatic than a harbour tour, a pleasure-boat trip on the broader waters of the Aussenalster is nevertheless highly recommended, revealing something of the elegant inner suburban areas, home to the city's wealthier inhabitants.**

The Harbour and Beyond

A stroll along the waterfront is an excellent way of beginning to absorb the atmosphere of this great city and understand the reasons for its existence. The **Landungsbrücken** are the pontoons at which ocean liners used to tie up; this trade has gone, but there's still plenty of activity on the broad waters of the

Elbe, as smaller craft mingle with the huge container ships making their way to and from the docks opposite. A cruise around the harbour in one of the many pleasure boats is an experience not to be missed, not least because of the views of Hamburg's distinctive skyline, dominated by the towers of the city's great churches. The highest at 132m (433ft) is that of the **St Michaelis-Kirche**, well worth the climb. Moored just to the east of the Landungsbrücken is the East India windjammer *Rickmer Rickmers*, a splendid reminder of the great days of sail. Further east still is the extraordinary conglomeration of 19th-century multi-storey red-brick warehouses known as the **Speicherstadt**, while 'inland' are the

Speicherstadt warehouses

Fleeten, the canals lined with merchants' dwellings which formed Hamburg's first harbour. The **Nikolaifleet** is the best preserved of them, while the Alsterfleet threads through the Altstadt (old town) into the **Binnenalster**, the smaller of the city's two lovely lakes. It passes close to the **Rathaus**, the monumental city hall built in 1897 in Northern Renaissance style, a striking symbol of Hamburg's confidence, pride and prosperity. Contemporary prosperity is much in evidence in the Alsterarkaden overlooking the Alsterfleet and in the other arcades and streets to the north.

Museums

Several of Hamburg's museums are grouped along the broad
semi-circular thoroughfare laid out along the line of the old
city walls, in particular along its eastern section, known as the
Museumsmeile (Museum Mile). The **Museum für Kunst
und Gewerbe** (Decorative Arts Museum; open Tues–Sun
10am–6pm, Thur until 9pm; admission fee) is one of the finest
and most comprehensive of its kind in Germany, with superlative exhibits ranging from medieval reliquaries to complete
Art Nouveau interiors; there's also a quite exceptional collection of antique keyboard instruments. The **Kunsthalle** (Art
Gallery; open Tues–Sun 10am–6pm, Thur until 9pm; admission fee) ranks among the country's leading galleries. Its
collection ranges from medieval times to the present, with
contemporary works housed in a spacious extension. The work
of 19th- and early 20th-century German artists is particularly
well represented. In the parkland at the western end of the old
city walls stands the **Museum für Hamburgische Geschichte** (City History Museum; open Tues–Sat 10am–5pm,
Sun 10am–6pm; admission fee), expertly evoking every aspect of Hamburg's past. The vast model railway, based on one
of the city's principal stations, amazes young and old alike.

St Pauli and the Reeperbahn

A rather different institution has an appropriate location in the
heart of the St Pauli red-light district, adjoining the **Landungsbrücken**; the **Erotic Art Museum** (open Sun–Thur
noon–10pm, Fri–Sat noon–midnight; admission fee) claims to
be the largest of its kind in the world, and treats its subject
with due seriousness and taste, with exhibits from the 6th century to the present. While St Pauli's main thoroughfare, the
Reeperbahn, certainly has its seedy side, its prostitutes, strip
shows and sex shops are complemented by the city's greatest
concentration of restaurants, bars, nightspots and other places

of entertainment, all of which make it a magnet for all sorts of folk simply wanting a good evening out. Those who have partied all Saturday night tend to congregate on Sunday morning at the waterside **Fischmarkt**, a boisterous affair where all sorts of merchandise, not only fish, is bought and sold.

Lübeck

Protected by formidable water defences, handsome **Lübeck** ◄ preserves the atmosphere of its glory days when it presided over the medieval Hanseatic League of trading cites and dominated the commerce of the Baltic and beyond. With no suitable stone at hand, the city was built of brick, and it was

Lübeck's Holstentor

here that *Backsteingotik* originated, a striking variant of Gothic architecture whose influence can be seen all round the Baltic shores, from Rostock to Tallinn in far-off Estonia. The style encompassed the humblest dwelling as much as the grandest church, and gave the Hansa cities their wonderfully harmonious appearance, none more so than Lübeck. Grievous wartime destruction – a single air raid in 1942 destroyed a quarter of the city – has been made good, and Lübeck more than deserves the UNESCO listing it was given in 1987.

The skills of Lübeck's builders are splendidly evident in the iconic structure guarding the main approach, the 15th-century gateway known as the **Holstentor**. Two sturdy brick towers are linked by a gatehouse containing an archway and topped by the typical stepped gables of *Backsteingotik*. Inside the gateway, the pride of the local history museum

Opposite the Marien-kirche is the Budden-brookhaus (open daily 10am–5pm; admission fee), a shrine to Lübeck's literary lion, Thomas Mann (1875–1955), whose most famous novel, *Buddenbrooks*, is set in the city.

(open Tues–Fri 10am–5pm, Sat–Sun 11am–5pm; admission fee) is a superb model of the city as it was in the 17th century. For a fine view over Lübeck and its setting near the mouth of the River Trave other than from the tower (open Apr–Oct daily 9am–7pm; admission fee) head to the nearby **Petrikirche**, whose viewing gallery is accessible by lift.

Almost always crowded, with both visitors and locals, the city's marketplace is dominated by the **Rathaus** (town hall) and the **Marienkirche**. The town hall's brickwork is extraordinarily elaborate, with dramatic circular openings in the upper walls to diminish wind resistance. The twin-towered church contains several works of art, and in one tower, two bells that crashed to the ground in the terrible air raid of 1942 have been left embedded in the floor of what is now a chapel as a memorial.

A stroll around the streets and squares reveals many minor treasures, among them the 13th-century hospice called the Heilig-Geist-Hospital, and the Haus der Schiffergesell-schaft, once the home of the sea-captains' guild and now a popular restaurant.

Lübeck is still a busy port, though its harbour is now at the mouth of the Trave. There, the elegant resort of **Trave-münde** boasts fine beaches, fishermen's houses, seafood restaurants and a casino.

Schleswig-Holstein and the North Sea Coast

Other resorts stud the Baltic coast to the north, whose most characteristic feature are lovely fjord-like inlets leading far inland to sheltered port towns.

The far north

The most important of these towns is Kiel, once Imperial Germany's most important naval base, and now the capital of the *Land* of Schleswig-Holstein, a peninsula stretching north to the border with Denmark. Kiel is famous for the world's greatest sailing event, the regatta known as the *Kieler Woche* (Kiel Week), and has also given its name (in English at least) to the great shipping canal linking the North Sea and the Baltic. At the head of other inlets stand the handsome towns of Schleswig and Flensburg. Schleswig's Renaissance Schloss Gottorf houses the Nydam Boat, a superb example of a Viking longship, while Flensburg, Germany's northernmost city, has a unique atmosphere thanks to its substantial Danish minority.

The great attraction of Germany's North Sea coastline is its islands. Forming two distinct groups, they consist of the **North Frisian Islands** stretching along the western coast of Schleswig-Holstein, and the **East Frisian Islands** off the coast of Lower Saxony. With sand dunes, abundant wildlife, glorious sandy beaches and fresh air guaranteed by the constant sea breeze, all are popular with visitors, though it is only North Frisian **Sylt** and its glamorous capital Westerland that are well known internationally. East Frisian Borkum and

Nordeney are equally bustling in summer, while smaller islands like Spiekeroog and Wangerooge are traffic-free and frequented by those who crave peace and quiet.

Between the two groups of Frisian islands, and quite unlike them, the island of **Helgoland** is buttressed by red sandstone cliffs. This one-time British possession lies about 70km (44 miles) offshore and is reached from the port of Cuxhaven at the mouth of the Elbe. Cuxhaven is overshadowed by far larger **Bremerhaven**, a modern harbour town first developed in the 19th century. A workaday place, it nevertheless attracts visitors to the magnificent **Deutsches Schiffahrtsmuseum** (National Maritime Museum; open Apr–Oct daily 10am–6pm, Nov–Mar Tues–Sun 10am–6pm; ad-

At the docks in Bremerhaven

mission fee), which deals expertly with all aspects of Germany's relationship with the sea. The star exhibit inside is a *Kogge*, the sturdy sailing ship that was the maid-of-all-work of the Hanseatic League. More historic vessels are moored outside, among them a U-boat. The **Zoo Am Meer Bremerhaven** (open Apr–Oct daily 9am–7pm, Nov–Mar daily 9am–4.30pm; admission fee) is a marine zoo specialising in Arctic fish and mammals.

Bremen

The ancient Hanseatic city of **Bremen** lies far inland up the River Weser. Like Hamburg,

The Bremen Town Musicians

Bremen is a Federal *Land* in its own right, and is equally proud of its history, which goes back to the 8th century. Overlooked by the twin-towered St Petri-Dom, parts of which date from the 11th century, the city's focal point is its sprawling square, at its centre the grandiose **Rathaus**, a splendid example of Weser Renaissance architecture. A huge medieval figure of the knight Roland, the guardian of civic liberties, stands in the square, contrasting with a droll modern sculpture which has become a city emblem: the Bremen Town Musicians (Stadtmusikanten; a cockerel, cat, dog and monkey, come from a folk tale popularised by the Brothers Grimm. The Weser waterfront with its bars and restaurants is reached from the square by the unusual Böttcherstrasse, a street laid out in the 1920s and 30s and flanked by brick buildings in Expressionist style. Among its shops and museums is the Paula Modersohn-Becker Museum, named after the best-known painter from the early 20th artists' colony established in the nearby village of Worpswede. Bremen's other most attractive street is the **Schnoorviertel**, the picturesque and much-tidied-up former fisherfolk's quarter.

Mecklenburg-Lower Pomerania

The lovely landscapes of the Mecklenburg lakeland begin within easy reach of Hamburg and Lübeck, and even **Schwerin**, the capital of the *Land* of Mecklenburg-Vorpommern is only a short distance away. Schwerin is an aristocratic place, the former seat of the dukes of Mecklenburg, with a charming Altstadt, a *Backsteingotik* cathedral, and a fabulous ducal palace on an island in the Schweriner See, Germany's third-largest lake. The **Schweriner Schloss** (open mid-Apr–mid-Oct Tues–Sun 10am–6pm, mid-Oct–mid-Apr 10am–5pm; admission fee) is a fantastical conglomeration of different architectural styles, from neo-Gothic to neo-baroque, with a tower, turret or pinnacle for every day of the year. As well as a sumptuous interior it has two superb gardens, the Burggarten and the Schlossgarten, the latter a masterpiece of baroque landscaping. East of Schwerin, the smaller, well-preserved town of **Güstrow** also has a ducal schloss, less ostentatious perhaps, but a fine example of genuine Renaissance architecture with a formal garden to match.

Linked to one another by rivers and canals, the countless waterbodies of the Mecklenburg lakeland are popular with

Müritzsee, largest of the Mecklenburg Lakes

Wismar

boating enthusiasts. The most extensive lake, second only to Lake Constance in size, is the **Müritzsee**, approached from the attractive town of Waren. Part of the area is protected as a national park, its woods, heaths and marshes a haven for wildlife, including Germany's heraldic bird, the sea eagle.

The Baltic Coast

Along the Baltic coast, splendid beaches and charmingly old-fashioned seaside resorts alternate with historic harbour towns. Like Lübeck, all the latter were once members of the Hanseatic League, and all share Lübeck's *Backsteingotik* atmosphere as well as having strong individual identities. **Wismar** is focused on its spacious marketplace, lined with gabled town mansions in various styles, at its centre the *Wassserkunst*, a domed Renaissance fountain. Beyond the one surviving city gateway is the Alter Hafen (Old Harbour), where a number of historic vessels are moored.

While Wismar was the GDR's second most important port, **Rostock** was promoted as the Communist state's main outlet to the world's oceans. A potential capital of Mecklenburg-Vorpommern, Rostock lost out in the end to Schwerin, but retains a livelier atmosphere than its competitor, particularly along its bustling main street, traffic-free Kröpeliner Strasse. Parallel to it runs Lange Strasse, a broad boulevard rebuilt after wartime bombing in a curious Stalinist version of *Backsteingotik*. Plenty of museums and monuments compete for the visitor's attention, perhaps the most interesting being the **Schiffahrtsmuseum** (Maritime Museum; open Tues–Sun

10am–6pm; admission fee), which traces the city's relationship with the Baltic, with particular emphasis on the GDR period. In summer, the best way of getting to Rostock's charming seaside suburb of **Warnemünde** with its promenade, cafés and restaurants, is by steamer along the wide River Warnow.

Some 70km (44 miles) to the east of Rostock and located on a superb natural harbour, compact **Stralsund** has kept more of its original character than the other port cities. Its great Marienkirche is physically linked to its Rathaus, an extraordinary edifice with a great seven-gabled façade. The town has a museum of more than local importance, the excellent **Deutsches Meeresmuseum** (National Museum of the Sea; open daily June–Sept 10am–6pm, Oct–May 10am–5pm; admission fee), which has no fewer than 45 aquariums. In recognition of their historical importance, Stralsund and Wismar have been given joint UNESCO World Heritage status.

Stralsund's distinctive town hall

The heyday of the Baltic coast as a summer resort was in the period before World War I and in the interwar years. But the groundwork had been laid much earlier by aristocrats: in the 1790s, Grand Duke Friedrich of Mecklenburg built a delightful group of neoclassical holiday villas at **Heiligendamm**, while the little spa town of **Putbus** was laid out in 1810 on **Rügen Island** by Prince Wilhelm Malte. Both are well preserved and can be enjoyed today. The chain of resorts (Bansin, Heringsdorf, Ahlbeck) fringing the glorious beaches of **Usedom**, Germany's easternmost island, are still proud to call themselves *Kaiserbäder* (Imperial spas), a status given them when they were patronised by Kaiser Wilhelm II and his court. Unlike the much redeveloped seaside resorts of western Germany, they and many of the other Baltic resorts have kept their period charm, with prettily decorated white villas, promenades and the occasional pier. Usedom's other great attraction is the **Historisch-Technische Informations-Zentrum** (open June–Sept daily 9am–6pm; Apr, May, Oct Tues–Sun 10am–6pm; Nov–Mar 10am–4pm; admission fee) at **Peenemünde**, the base where the deadly V2 rocket was developed in World War II.

Rügen Island, which is reached from Stralsund, is Germany's largest island, with a wealth of things to visit, among them the **Nationalpark Jasmund**, with its gorgeous forests of beech and the sparkling white chalk cliffs immortalised in a famous painting by the early 19th-century artist Caspar David Friedrich.

Live Steam

Steam railways are very much alive in the former GDR, many of them having been preserved for their usefulness and not just for sentimental reasons. Holidaymakers on Rügen Island are carried around by 'Rasender Roland' (Rushing Roland), while 'Molli' steams through the streets of the spa of Bad Doberan on its way to the coastal resorts of Heiligdamm and Kühlungsborn. There are also several steam railways in Saxony. But the most impressive steam line of all is the 110-km (70-mile) Harz railway, a branch of which chugs valiantly all the way to the summit of the Brocken mountain *(see page 76)*.

View over Saxony's 'Little Switzerland', near Dresden

DRESDEN AND THE TWO SAXONYS

Until 1918 Saxony, like Bavaria, was a kingdom, and today's *Land* retains a strong sense of itself as a realm of some distinction, calling itself *Freistaat Sachsen* (the Free State of Saxony). The Saxon rulers were renowned for their extravagant love of the arts, and their capital Dresden, with its great monuments lovingly rebuilt after wartime devastation, once more deserves its title of 'Florence on the Elbe'. Just downstream from Dresden, the much smaller but almost perfectly preserved little city of Meissen was where a Saxon king's obsession with fine things led to the discovery of the secret of porcelain manufacture. The wealth and fame of Saxony's second great city, Leipzig, was created not by monarchs but by merchants, publishers, printers and musicians, foremost among the latter Johann Sebastian Bach. In 1989, it was here that the wave of popular protest gathered strength that led to the downfall of the Communist regime.

Saxony has fine countryside, particularly in the upland areas along the border with the Czech Republic. Here, the Erzgebirge (Ore Mountains) are the home of long-standing mining traditions, while few of Germany's landscapes are as spectacular as the 300-m (1,000-ft) cliffs and rock formations towering over the Elbe in the national park known as Saxony's 'Little Switzerland' (Sächsische Schweiz).

The 'other Saxony', Sachsen-Anhalt, is a recent creation as a *Land*. Its capital, Magdeburg, has eastern Germany's finest medieval cathedral, while its rival, Halle, is proud of its musical traditions as well as boldly facing up to the problematic industrial heritage bequeathed by Communism. Dessau is famous as the home of the influential interwar Bauhaus school of design, while nearby is the World Heritage Site of Wörlitz, Germany's foremost landscape park.

Dresden

Demoted by the Communists to a mere district town, princely **Dresden** is once more the capital of Saxony. While the city will never quite recover the allure it had before the Allied air raids of February 1945, the reconstruction of its great historic buildings has restored its famous skyline and its unparalleled artistic heritage draws visitors from all over the world.

Near the River

Perhaps the best place to begin an exploration of Dresden's wealth of attractions is to stroll along the **Brühlsche Terrasse**, the elevated promenade laid out along the banks of the Elbe. The terrace gives wonderful views of the river, graced by the big white pleasure steamers of the famous *Weisse Flotte* (White Fleet). On the far shore is the Neustadt, the elegant 18th-century town extension which was relatively unaffected by the bombing, and which now attracts the crowds to its shops, cafés, restaurants and nightlife. By the

The Dresden skyline at the Brühlsche Terrasse

Altstadt end of the Augustusbrücke, the bridge named after Augustus the Strong, Saxony's most flamboyant monarch, stands the lovely **Hofkirche**, the baroque court church. It was designed by an Italian architect, who imported numerous fellow-countrymen to help in its construction, housing them in the **Italienisches Dörfchen** (Italian Village), now a popular riverside restaurant. The church abuts the **Residenzschloss** (open Wed–Mon 10am–6pm; admission fee), until 1918 the palace of Saxony's kings. With rebuilding almost complete, it now houses some of the city's most important collections, among them the **Kupferstichkabinett** (Museum of Prints and Drawings) with its half-a-million prints, drawings and photographs, and the **Grünes Gewölbe** (Green Vault), a sumptuous array of decorative objects on which Augustus squandered his kingdom's wealth. There's a fine panorama over the city centre from the palace's 100-m (328-ft) tower (open summer Tues–Sun 10am–6pm; admission fee).

The opulent Zwinger

Central Dresden

On the far side of the Theaterplatz stands the **Semperoper** (Opera House), named after its architect, Gottfried Semper, and the scene of many a prestigious premiere, including operas by Wagner. Adjoining it is the **Zwinger**, perhaps the most stunning group of baroque buildings in Germany. Arranged around a spacious courtyard with lawns, pools and fountains, the Zwinger was built from 1709 onwards by Augustus's architect Pöppelmann to house the spendthrift monarch's collections and to be an appropriate setting for ostentatious pageants and festivities. The collections (open Tues–Sun 10am–6pm; admission fee) include the **Gemäldegalerie Alte Meister** (Old Masters' Gallery), which houses some of the world's finest paintings including Raphael's emblematic *Sistine Madonna*; the fabulous **Porzellansammlung** (Porcelain Collection) and the **Rüstkammer** (Armoury); and the antique scientific instruments of the **Mathematisch-Physikalischer Salon** (Mathematical-Physical Sciences Saloon).

The counterpart to the Old Masters' Gallery is the **Galerie Neue Meister** (New Masters' Gallery; open Wed–Mon 10am–6pm; admission fee) in the **Albertinum**; here are works by some of Germany's greatest 19th- and 20th-century artists, among them one of the most searing condemnations of war ever painted, the triptych *Der Krieg* by Otto Dix. Symbolising Dresden's recovery from the horrors of war is the glorious domed **Frauenkirche** (Church of Our Lady), for decades a ruin, then rebuilt stone by numbered stone from 1994 onwards, and finally reconsecrated in late 2005. The gilded cross atop the dome was donated by Britain's 'Dresden Trust'.

The area around the Frauenkirche is scheduled to be rebuilt along traditional lines, respecting the old, irregular street pattern. By contrast, much of the postwar reconstruction of war-wrecked Dresden paid little attention to history, and the main shopping area, traffic-free **Prager Strasse**, is a Communist-era showpiece of unrelenting geometric regularity.

Outer Dresden

Some of the atmosphere of the prewar city lingers in the elegant villa quarters of the suburbs and in open spaces such as the vast **Grosser Garten**, one of Germany's foremost urban parks. On the edge of the park is one of the country's most unusual museums, the **Deutsches Hygiene-Museum** (open Tues–Sun 10am–6pm; admission fee), its most prized exhibit the 'Glass Human', with a completely transparent body. Some of the loveliest vistas of Dresden are from the heights above the River Elbe just upstream from the centre; they can be reached from the suburb of Loschwitz by funicular and cable railway.

Around Dresden

The impact of Augustus the Strong was felt far beyond the city limits. His pleasure palaces in the countryside around Dresden include the huge hunting lodge of **Schloss Moritzburg** (open daily 10am–5.30pm in summer, restricted hours in winter; admission fee), 14km (9 miles) northwest of Dresden. Rising from the middle of a great artificial lake on which lavish water pageants were held, it has an interior crammed with trophies of the chase. Upstream from the city and best reached by pleasure steamer, the mock-Chinese extravaganza of **Schloss Pillnitz** (open May–Oct daily 10am–6pm; admission fee) stands among the vineyards rising from the riverbank. It makes a fine home for a superlative decorative arts collection.

The steamer continues upstream from Pillnitz to the small historic town of **Pirna**, then passes beneath the most spectacular feature of the national park of **Sächische Schweiz** (Saxony's 'Little Switzerland'), the cliffs, crags and pinnacles of the **Bastei** rock. The panorama from the Bastei, with its catwalks and vertiginous viewpoints, is one of the most sensational in Germany, taking in the winding river far below as well as other imposing rock formations,

---

The Sorbs

Visitors to southeastern Germany are sometimes surprised to find bilingual road signs, pointing, for example, to Bautzen – Budyšin. The latter is the name used for the city by the Sorbs, a Slav minority of some 50,000 people who have somehow managed to preserve their language and culture despite being surrounded and overwhelmingly outnumbered by Germans. Colourful Sorbian traditions include Zapust, several days of festivities at Shrovetide, while Easter is marked by horseback processions and intricately painted Easter eggs.

one of them crowned by the great fortress of **Königstein**.

Most trippers leave the steamer at the spa town of **Bad Schandau**, though it is sometimes possible to carry on upstream into the Czech Republic. Less dramatic than Saxon Switzerland, but still with many charms, the well-wooded upland countryside along the Czech border is a paradise for walkers and the less ambitious winter sports enthusiast. Known as the **Lausitz**, and once part of the

Meissen

Czech kingdom, it has its own miniature capital in the shape of **Bautzen**. This 1,000-year-old, many-towered city built above the winding River Spree is the main cultural centre of the Sorb minority, and its castle, the Ortenburg, is the home of the Serbski Musej (Sorbian Museum; open daily 10am–5pm; admission fee). Bautzen was notorious for its harsh prison, the **Gedenkstätte Bautzen** (open Tues–Sun 10am–4pm), now a memorial to people who suffered under successive regimes.

Separated from Poland only by the River Neisse, **Görlitz**, 39km (24 miles) east of Bautzen, miraculously survived World War II with little damage. Its extensive Altstadt, which features wonderful medieval churches and Renaissance mansions, is one of the best preserved in Germany.

Downstream along the Elbe from Dresden, **Meissen** is dominated by its cathedral and castle, the **Albrechtsburg**, built on the rocky bluff overlooking the river. It was while confined to the castle that Augustus's court alchemist discovered the technique of making perfect porcelain. The streets, squares and alleyways of the old town are a delight to explore, but most visitors come here for the **Staatliche Porzellan-Manufaktur** (State Porcelain Factory; open daily 9am–6pm, until 5pm in winter; admission fee), to see craftspeople at work and marvel at the historic porcelain in the museum.

Colditz Castle (open Apr–Oct Mon–Fri 9am–5pm, Sat–Sun 10am–4pm; Nov–Mar Mon–Fri 9am–4pm; admission fee) is just one of several ancient strongholds along the picturesque River Mulde, but owes its near-mythical status to its role as a prison for incorrigible Allied escapers in World War II. A tour reveals the extraordinary ingenuity of those confined here, 30 of whom succeeded in making 'home runs' from the supposedly escape-proof fortress.

Leipzig's Thomaskirche, with Bach's statue

Leipzig

Mercantile **Leipzig** makes little attempt to compete with princely Dresden in terms of glamour and great monuments. It's a workaday city, whose historic buildings reflect civic pride rather than aristocratic ambition. Typical is the **Altes Rathaus** (Old Town Hall; open Tues–Sun 10am–6pm; admission fee), with its steep roof, clock tower and distinctive gables. Run up astonishingly quickly in the space of a few months in 1556 in the interval between two of Leipzig's famous trade fairs, it now houses the city museum and a superb ceremonial hall graced by portraits of city fathers.

All around are the arcades which have long been a feature of Leipzig; once used to display the wares of merchants attending the fairs, they now make it possible to shop your way around the city almost entirely under cover. In one of the arcades, the **Mädlerpassage**, is **Auerbachs Keller**, the vaulted basement pub which was the scene of a dramatic episode in Goethe's *Faust*. Goethe had many connections with Leipzig, and his statue stands in the Naschmarkt in front of the old stock exchange, the city's loveliest baroque building.

But the man most people associate with Leipzig has to be Johann Sebastian Bach. In 1723 Bach was appointed city musician and choirmaster of the 13th century **Thomaskirche** (Church of St Thomas). The celebrated boys' choir, the Thomaner, still sing. Their former master is buried in his church, and his statue stands outside, opposite the **Bachmuseum** (open daily 10am–5pm; admission fee).

As well as the Thomaskirche, Leipzig has another landmark church, the **Nikolaikirche** (Church of St Nicholas), a Romanesque structure given a highly original, gloriously ornate interior in the late 18th century. In the 1980s, it served as a refuge for opponents of the GDR regime, and in 1989 it was the rallying point for the great demonstrations which led to the government's collapse. The story of what Leipzig's resisters

Bach's works were neglected after his death, and the revival of his reputation only came during the 19th century, thanks to the efforts of Felix Mendelssohn, who conducted Leipzig's renowned Gewandhaus orchestra between 1835 and 1845. With its fine acoustics, today's Gewandhaus building is one of the more distinguished edifices of the Communist era.

were up against is compellingly told in the **Museum in der 'runden Ecke'** (Museum in the 'Round Corner'; open daily 10am–6pm; free), the former Stasi secret police headquarters, while the daily realities of life under Communism are evoked in the excellent displays of the **Zeitgeschichtliches Forum** (Contemporary History Forum; open Tues–Fri 9am–6pm, Sat–Sun 10am–6pm; free).

There's plenty more to see in Leipzig; if you have come here by train, you will already have admired the huge railway station, said to be the largest terminus in the world. Even more colossal is the granite **Völkerschlachtdenkmal** (open Apr–Oct daily 10am–6pm, Nov–Mar 10am–4pm; admission fee), the monument to the Battle of the Nations, which took place outside the city in 1813. Erected exactly a century later, this man-made mountain is the perfect embodiment of the bombastic, militaristic spirit of Kaiser Wilhelm's Germany.

The Kornhaus restaurant in Dessau

Lutherstadt Wittenberg

The Leipzig–Berlin train pauses briefly at **Lutherstadt Wittenberg**, an otherwise modest town so proud of its associations with Martin Luther that it has incorporated his name into its official title. It was here that Luther nailed his 95 theses to the church door, and there are many sights connected with him, foremost among them the **Lutherhalle** (open Apr–Oct daily 9am–6pm, Nov–Mar Tues–Sun 10am–

Bauhaus main building, Dessau

5pm; admission fee), with its museum of the Reformation. In the middle of the UNESCO Biosphere Reserve along the Elbe downstream from Wittenberg spreads the parkland of **Wörlitz**, laid out in the late 18th century for Prince Leopold of Anhalt-Dessau. It is perhaps Germany's supreme achievement in landscape design, with lakes, pavilions, gazebos, romantic ruins and lavish planting.

Prince Leopold and the other rulers of Anhalt-Dessau beautified their capital, **Dessau**, which was devastated in World War II. The city is remembered today mostly as the seat of the hugely influential design school of the interwar period, the **Bauhaus**. Its pioneering main building, all glass, steel and concrete, designed by Walter Gropius, still stands, a magnet for design students and enthusiasts from all over the world. Among Dessau's other examples of Modernist architecture are the **Meisterhäuser**, cuboid residences built for the Bauhaus professors and, on the banks of the Elbe, the panoramic **Kornhaus** restaurant.

Magdeburg and Halle

Astride the River Elbe and the main routes from western Germany to Berlin, **Magdeburg** enjoys a favourable location which may have been decisive when it was chosen as the capital of Sachsen-Anhalt against fierce competition from Halle. The city's origins go back to the early Middle Ages, when the Elbe was the frontier between Germans and Slavs, and Magdeburg became a great centre of German-Christian missionary work and conquest. Little remains of the historic town, destroyed in successive sieges and wars, but over everything still rises the superb twin-towered **Dom**, a Gothic structure with an interior rich in sculpture of all periods.

Magdeburg's rival, **Halle**, 29km (18 miles) to the northwest of Leipzig, is the larger of the two cities, a bustling place centred on its irregular Marktplatz dominated by the landmark Roter Turm (Red Tower) and the four spires of the Marktkirche. The city's most famous son, Georg Friedrich Händel, played the organ here, and his life and work are celebrated in his birthplace, the **Händel-Haus** (open Mon, Wed, Fri 9.30am–5.30pm; Thur, Sat, Sun 9.30am–7pm; admission fee). Halle's notoriously polluting chemical industries have either gone out of business or been cleaned up; their origins go back centuries to the discovery of saline springs, and an intriguing and unusual attraction is the old saltworks, now the **Technisches Halloren und Salinenmuseum** (open Tues–Sun 10am–5pm; admission fee).

WEIMAR AND THURINGIA

At the geographical heart of Germany, the *Land* of Thüringen (Thuringia) seems to distil the very essence of the country. Stately old towns are strung along the Via Regia, the ancient highway leading east–west across the province; there are ancient castles and churches galore, while to the south stretch the wonderfully wooded uplands of the Thuringian Forest.

The Wartburg, Thuringia's mighty stronghold

Productive farming countryside abounds, and, just over the border in Sachsen-Anhalt, vineyards flourish along the picturesque course of the River Saale. While the capital of classical German culture, Weimar, has always drawn visitors from around the globe, the rest of Thuringia has remained relatively unknown. Nowadays, however, more and more people are discovering its manifold attractions.

Weimar

This modest little city still seems to breathe the harmonious atmosphere of the golden age in Germany's cultural history known as Weimar Classicism. The place is indissolubly associated with the name of that universal genius, Johann Wolfgang von Goethe (1749–1832), who for most of his life served as a privy councillor of Carl August, enlightened ruler of the little duchy of Saxony-Weimar-Eisenach. Goethe attracted other luminaries here like his friend and fellow playwright Friedrich Schiller. Other figures who flourished at Weimar, both before and after Goethe's time, include the painter Cranach the Elder, the poet Christoph-Martin Wieland, and the philosopher Johann Gottfried Herder. Bach was court musician for a while, as was Liszt, and Nietzsche spent the last part of his life in Weimar. In 1919 the Bauhaus design school started here, and the city gave its name to the ill-fated interwar Weimar Republic, whose parliament drew up its democratic constitution here at a safe distance from Berlin, which was racked by revolutionary disturbance.

Weimar has no grandiose monuments, and the best way to experience the town is to wander its streets at random, perhaps beginning at the **Deutsches Nationaltheater** (German National Theatre), fronted by a famous statue of Goethe and Schiller. One compulsory stop is **Goethe's Wohnhaus** (Goethe's House; open Apr–Sept Tues–Sun 9am–6pm, Oct–Mar Tues–Sun 9am–4pm; admission fee). The original house, with its many poignant reminders of the great man, is adjoined by an excellent modern museum devoted to his life and times. Goethe was fascinated by landscape, and helped lay out the lovely **Park an der Ilm** with its little retreat known as **Goethes Gartenhaus**.

About 8km (5 miles) to

Goethe and Schiller in Weimar

the north of the city is **Buchenwald** concentration camp, established by the Nazis in 1937. Named after the area's abundant beechwoods, Buchenwald was not an extermination camp as such, though by the end of World War II more than 50,000 people had perished here. A further 10,000 deaths occurred in the immediate postwar period. The remains of the camp are now the **Gedenkstätte Buchenwald** (Buchenwald Memorial; open May–Sept Tues–Sun 9.45am–6pm, Oct– Apr Tues–Sun 8.45am–5pm).

Erfurt, Gotha and Eisenach

The Via Regia leads westwards from Weimar to well-preserved **Erfurt**, the capital of Thuringia and one of the great cities of medieval Germany. Among the many things to see is the **Krämerbrücke** (Merchants' Bridge), a medieval river crossing lined with shops, but the most striking sight in Erfurt is that of its two great churches looming high above the spacious Domplatz; the **Severikirche** with its spiky steeples is impressive enough, but the cathedral's proportions are truly stunning. Its treasures include the huge

Weimar Classicism

That size really doesn't matter is proved by the way in which little Weimar with its tiny ducal court became the cultural capital of Germany in the late 18th and early 19th century. The genial figures of Schiller and Goethe bestrode the intellectual currents of the age, producing literature that, like Shakespeare's works, is of universal appeal and significance and cannot be contained within any single category. As well as a prodigious output of poetry, novels and plays like *Faust*, Goethe made valuable contributions to the natural sciences, while Schiller is best known for historical dramas like *Maria Stuart* which have recently enjoyed a revival in English translation.

Gloriosa bell, superb stained glass and a triangular porch adorned with sculptures of the Wise and Foolish Virgins.

Further along the east–west highway stands the little city of **Gotha**, once the seat of the Saxe-Coburg-Gotha dynasty which provided monarchs for much of Europe, including Britain, and which gave its name to the *Who's Who* of German aristocracy, the *Almanac de Gotha*. The charming old town with its delightful red Renaissance Rathaus crouches at the foot of the rise crowned by gigantic **Schloss Friedenstein** (open Tues–Sun 10am–5pm, until 4pm in winter; admission fee). Built in the mid-17th century, the great ducal residence with its formidable corner towers has a sumptuous interior housing the extensive collections assembled by successive dukes, as well as an original baroque theatre.

The westernmost of Thuringia's string of cities, almost on the border with Hessen, **Eisenach** attracts visitors in

The cathedral (left) and Severikirche in Erfurt

their thousands. Most come here to marvel at the **Wartburg** (open Mar–Oct daily 8.30am–5pm, Nov–Feb daily 9am–3.30pm; admission fee), the 11th-century stronghold perched atop the last spur of the Thuringian Forest above the town. Everyone's idea of what a German castle should be like, the Wartburg is rich in romantic associations and in the 19th century became a great symbol of German nationalism, when it was zealously (perhaps over-zealously) restored. Earlier it had been a refuge for Martin Luther, who completed his translation of the Bible here; a mark on the wall of his study is supposed to be the result of his hurling his inkpot at the devil.

Eisenach's Automobil-baumuseum (Car Museum; open Tues–Sun 10am–5pm; admission fee) reflects the city's long association with car manufacturing. Exhibits include the nearest thing the GDR had to a prestige vehicle, the Wartburg.

Luther is remembered in Eisenach itself, where he lodged as a schoolboy in what is now the **Luther-Haus** (open Apr–Oct daily 9am–5pm, Nov–Mar daily 10am–5pm; admission fee) and where he later preached in the Georgenkirche. But the city's most famous son is Bach, born in the **Bach-Haus** (open daily 10am–6pm; admission fee), now 600 years old, which has a fine collection of antique musical instruments.

Thuringian Forest

There are fine views of the forested uplands of the **Thuringian Forest** or **Thüringer Wald** from Wartburg Castle, as well as from the nearby **Burschenschaftsdenkmal** (Fraternities Memorial), erected to mark a great rally of patriotic students in 1817. One of central Germany's favourite holiday and recreation areas, the Thuringian Forest rises to a height of nearly 1,000m (3,280ft) near the ski resort of Oberhof, but the best vistas are from the Grosser

Inselberg, 916m (3,005ft) high above the little summer resort and spa of Tabarz. Keen hikers will tackle the famous long-distance trail of the **Rennweg**, a ridge-walk running the whole 100-km (60-mile) length of the forest, while admirers of Goethe will want to follow in his footsteps to the countryside he loved around the old town of **Ilmenau**.

Arising in the eastern part of the Thuringian Forest, and with its upper reaches marked by a series of dams and reservoirs, the River Saale winds its way past picturesque small towns like **Saalfeld** and **Rudolstadt**. Close to Saalfeld are caves with astonishing concretions, the **Feengrotten** (Fairy Grottoes; open Mar–Oct daily 9am–5pm, Nov Sat–Sun 10am–3.30pm, Dec–Feb daily 10am–3.30pm; admission fee), considered to be the most colourful in the world.

The Saale flows north to the city of **Jena**, Thuringia's scientific counterpart to literary Weimar, as much identified with the 19th-century optical genius Carl Zeiss as the latter is with Goethe. Dominated by the cylindrical skyscraper of the university, Jena is still very much a centre of the optical and other hi-tech industries, whose origins are traced in the **Optisches Museum** (Museum of Optics; open Tues–Fri 10am–4.30pm, Sat 1–4pm; admission fee). Continuing northwards over the border into Sachsen-Anhalt, the Saale is joined by its tributary the Unstrut.

The valley's combination of suitable soils and a favourable microclimate explains the presence here of Europe's northernmost vineyard, centred on the charming little wine town of Freyberg and on the larger cathedral city of **Naumburg**. Its distinctive four-towered profile visible from far away, Naumburg's Dom is a splendid synthesis of Romanesque and Gothic architecture, though its great fame rests on its sculptures, particularly the noble couple known as Ekkehardt and Uta, the embodiment of the Germanic ideal of medieval chivalry.

View of the Harz Mountains, towards the Brocken

HANOVER AND THE HARZ

While the great commercial and industrial city of Hanover wears a resolutely modern face, and is more famous for its trade fairs than its historic heritage, this region of central Germany has a wealth of ancient and well-preserved towns. Hameln (Hamelin), whose children were spirited away by the sound of the Ratcatcher's flute, is a delight, as is timber-framed Goslar, the gateway to the Harz, the country's highest range of mountains north of the Alps, much of which is designated a national park. Less spectacular, the low-lying countryside north of Hanover includes the rolling, sandy expanses of Lüneburg Heath, bounded by the fine old cities of Lüneburg and Celle.

Hanover

The capital of the *Land* of Lower Saxony (Niedersachsen), and the former seat of the dynasty that gave England a royal line in the 18th century, Hanover no longer has a princely

Hanover's Neues Rathaus

palace, thanks to bombing in World War II. But its **Grosser Garten** (Great Garden) survives; it is one of the great glories of baroque landscape design, linked to other historic parks (known collectively as the Herrenhausen gardens) by an avenue of lime trees and featuring a fountain spurting a jet of water 80m (260ft) into the air. On the far, southeastern side of the rebuilt city centre, there is another kind of open space, even more popular with locals: the **Maschsee**; its broad waters make a fine foil to Hanover's most prominent public building, the **Neues Rathaus** (New City Hall). Completed in 1913, it has a flamboyant, neo-baroque exterior concealing opulent Art Nouveau interiors. The tower can be ascended by an inclined elevator for an overall view of the city in its green setting. Postwar Hanover profited from Leipzig's disappearance behind the Iron Curtain to become West Germany's leading centre of trade fairs, the extensive grounds of which have their own mainline rail station. The city's status was enhanced by the international Expo held here in 2000, Germany's first.

Hameln and Hildesheim
South of Hanover, the valley of the winding River Weser leads upstream through ever more attractive countryside.

The river has given its name to a style of architecture known as 'Weser Renaissance', nowhere more splendidly exemplified than in **Hameln**, its old streets lined with exuberantly decorated, high-gabled town mansions. Better known in English as Hamelin, the town stages a weekly pageant celebrating the story of the infamous *Rattenfänger*, the stranger who rid the town first of its rats, then, when the city fathers withheld his fee, of its children.

There's more fine architecture in **Hildesheim**, though virtually every building on its Marktplatz is a reconstruction following near-total wartime destruction. But the town's greatest treasure is its heritage of Romanesque church architecture, protected by a UNESCO World Heritage designation. It includes the perfectly preserved Godehardikirche, the Michaeliskirche with its painted ceiling, and the Dom, with its extraordinary 11th-century bronze doors depicting episodes from the Old and New Testaments.

Harz Mountains

Visitors heading for the mountains of the Harz are strongly recommended to take a break in the old Imperial town of **Goslar**. A stroll around the cobbled streets reveals ever-changing compositions formed by an array of 1,000 or so ancient dwellings, most of them timber-framed and many featuring a wealth of carved detail. None is more charming than the imposing early 16th-century magistrate's residence known as the Brusttuch, now a hotel. Of a different order altogether is the Kaiserpfalz,

For 1,000 years, the Harz Mountains were exploited for their mineral wealth, yielding quantities of copper, lead, tin, zinc, silver and gold. The region's mining traditions can be investigated in the Bergbaumuseum Rammelsberg (Mining Museum; open daily 9am–6pm), just outside Goslar.

the Imperial palace originally erected in the 11th century and comprehensively restored in the 1870s as a symbol of the newly united German Empire.

Visitors come to the Harz for the region's fresh air, hiking trails and broad vistas. Nowhere is the panorama more spectacular than from the rounded summit of the **Brocken**, at 1,142m (3,747ft) the highest point in central Germany. The Brocken features strongly in German myth, legend and literature, not least because of the way Goethe evoked its Walpurgisnacht *(see below)* in his *Faust*. The mountain can be admired from the popular viewpoint of Torfhaus, where there is a national park information centre. Any number of trails lead to the summit; the easy way up is by the narrow-gauge trains of the Brockenbahn, hauled by magnificent steam engines built specially for this demanding job. In GDR times, the Brocken was forbidden territory, with the Stasi deploying elaborate listening equipment able to pick up capitalist conversations hundreds of kilometres away. Their spying paraphernalia has been succeeded by the Brockenhaus, a museum explaining the history and ecology of the mountain. An easy walk leads

Walpurgisnacht

In the Harz, the hours before dawn on 1 May are known as 'Walpurgis Night' or the 'Witches' Sabbath'. Legend has it that this is the time when witches gather on the Hexentanzplatz above Thale, before flying to the top of the Brocken on brooms, dung-forks and even tomcats. Here they dance wildly with each other before mating with the Devil, who confirms their magic powers. The legend gained credibility when Goethe made use of it in *Faust*, and nowadays the eve of Mayday is celebrated with abandon in towns and villages all around the Harz by thousands of costumed 'devils' and 'witches'.

round the summit, past strange rock formations where witches are said to consort with the Devil.

There are plenty of pleasant resorts in and around the Harz, but perhaps more interesting are towns like **Wernigerode**, with its timber-framed buildings and extraordinarily picturesque old town hall. To the southeast is the rather run-down industrial town of Thale, a base for exploration of the rocky ravine of the River Bode, which penetrates the very heart of the mountains. High above the gorge is the Hexentanzplatz (Witches' Dancing Place) viewpoint, reached by a short but spectacular trip in a cable-car.

In the flat agricultural country to the east of the mountains stands **Quedlinburg**. Few places exude quite the same sense of Germany's deep history as this small town, overlooked by its Burgberg, the hilltop citadel whose church contains a fabulous treasury and the tomb of King Heinrich I, the country's

Picturesque Quedlinburg

earliest king. The stone and timber-framed houses lining the lanes and streets below make up one of the finest collections of medieval and later buildings in the country. The whole of old Quedlinburg is deservedly a UNESCO World Heritage Site.

Around Lüneburg Heath

About 50km (30 miles) to the northwest of Hanover is the **Lüneburg Heath** or **Lüneburger Heide**, a vast tract of what was once continuous forest, but which human activity has converted over the centuries into a mosaic of farmland, woodland, marshland and pastureland grazed by a unique breed of sheep. Sections of the area are protected as nature parks, and the heath has become increasingly popular with walkers, riders and wildlife enthusiasts. The Nazis located one of their more notorious concentration camps here; the liberation of **Bergen-Belsen** in early 1945 brought home to

Heather on the Lüneburg Heath

the world the horrors of the Nazi regime. The camp, located on the west side of the Heath, is now a memorial site.

Celle, at the southern edge of the Heath, was a ducal seat and wears an aristocratic air. Its Schloss (open Apr–Oct Tues–Sun for hourly guided tours 11am–3pm, Nov–Mar tours at 11am, 3pm; admission fee) contains a lovely Renaissance chapel and a baroque theatre. With a heritage of hundreds of fine timber-framed dwellings, the town is also graced by a Rathaus in exuberant Weser Renaissance style. Celle is the German capital of equestrianism, the home of the State Stud Farm of Lower Saxony and of a splendid September parade of stallions.

North of the Heath and close to Hamburg, the town of **Lüneburg** is well worth a visit, its fine brick buildings reflecting its past connections with the Hansa cities of the coast. The town's prosperity depended on its salt deposits, and the old salt works have been converted into the Deutsches Salzmuseum (National Salt Museum; open Apr–Sept daily 9am–5pm, Oct–Mar daily 10am–5pm; admission fee).

Lemgo

Just over the border in the *Land* of North-Rhine Westfalia, **Lemgo** was spared wartime damage and ranks among the most picturesque of the country's smaller towns, with an outstanding roster of late medieval and early Renaissance dwellings. Among them is the Hexenbürgermeisterhaus (House of the Witches' Mayor), home to a 16th-century mayor horribly zealous in his pursuit of witches; he sent dozens of innocent women to their death. Not far from Lemgo, the hills of the Teutoburger Wald are said to be the site of the great battle of AD9 in which the German chieftain Hermann won a great victory over the Roman legions sent against him. A gigantic 19th-century stone figure of Germany's first national hero rises from a summit, his mighty sword fashioned from steel supplied by the Krupp armament works.

Cologne Cathedral and restored Altstadt at night

COLOGNE, THE RUHR AND RHINE

The westernmost part of Germany is one of the most densely populated parts of the country. The great cities like Cologne and Düsseldorf, and the industrial centres of the Ruhr, all have their own distinct identities and range of attractions. Once the boundary of the Roman Empire, the Rhine remains one of Germany's great tourist attractions, especially where it has cut a spectacular winding gorge between Bingen and Koblenz. The valley of the Mosel is hardly less scenic. Less dramatic, the flat and watery landscapes around Münster, the old capital of Westphalia, invite quiet exploration.

Cologne

A great city in Roman times, and, in the Middle Ages, Germany's largest, **Cologne** is dominated by its glorious twin-towered cathedral, one of the supreme achievements of Gothic architecture. Repeatedly bombed in World War II,

Cologne preserved its historic street pattern when it was re-built and, although most buildings are modern, much of its traditional atmosphere survives. It's a lively, humorous, rather disrespectful place, best experienced – for those with stamina – during the merrymaking of Karneval time *(see page 83)*. The historic core of Cologne is large, bounded by the semi-circular boulevard of the *Ring* running along the line of the old city walls, but the epicentre of city life is in the busy squares around the cathedral and the main railway station, one of the country's largest.

Kölner Dom and the Altstadt

Although construction of **Kölner Dom** (Cologne Cathedral; open Mon–Fri 10am–6.30pm, Sat 10am–5pm, Sun 1–5pm; admission fee to tower) began in the 13th century, the building was only completed at the end of the 19th century, albeit in faithful adherence to the original medieval drawings which had somehow survived. The steeples rise to an astonishing 157m (515ft), and it takes more than 500 steps to reach the viewing platform on the south tower. The interior too aston-ishes with its huge scale, as well as with a fabulous array of ecclesiastical treasures; they include the poignant 10th-century Cross of Gero show-ing Christ at the moment of death, the incredibly ornate Shrine of the Three Magi, and an altar painting by Cologne's greatest medieval painter, Stefan Lochner.

Shrine of the Three Magi

Flanking the cathedral's south front is the **Römisch-Germanisches Museum** (Roman-Germanic Museum;

Karneval reveller

open Tues–Sun 10am–5pm; admission fee). Well displayed items tell the story of this important frontier outpost of the Roman Empire, prominent among them the Dionysus Mosaic, made up of more than a million pieces and one of the finest of its kind anywhere.

From near the cathedral, Hohe Strasse follows the course of a Roman road southwards. Between it and the Rhine stretches the restored Altstadt, with its countless pubs, bars and restaurants, as well as surviving monuments like the Rathaus with its medieval towers, the Jewish *Mikwe* or ritual bath, and Gross St Martin, one of the city's many fine Romanesque churches. At the heart of the Altstadt is the postmodern structure housing the splendid **Wallraf-Richartz-Museum** (open Tues 10am–8pm, Wed–Fri 10am–6pm, Sat–Sun 11am– 6pm; admission fee), whose prize exhibits are pictures by the late-medieval painters of the Cologne School, among them Lochner's masterpiece, the exquisite *Madonna in the Rose Garden*.

The city's other great art gallery is the vast **Museum Ludwig** (open Tues–Thur, Sat–Sun 10am–6pm, Fri 11am–6pm; admission fee) overlooking the Rhine. It's one of the best galleries of modern art in Germany, and its collection of American painting – Warhol, Rothko, Rauschenberg – is un-

surpassed. A walkway leads from here along the great railway bridge over the Rhine, giving an unbeatable view of the
city's waterfront and the elaborate eastern end of the cathedral.

Two of Cologne's more unusual museums are the Imhoff-
Stollwerck-Museum (open Tues–Fri 10am–6pm, Sat–Sun
11am–7pm; admission fee), devoted to chocolate, and the
Deutsches Sport- und Olympia-Museum (National Sport and
Olympics Museum; open Tues–Fri 10am–6pm, Sat–Sun
11am–7pm; admission fee) with plenty of interactive exhibits.

Brühl

Only a short distance from Cologne, the town of **Brühl** offers
contrasting possibilities for a day out. **Phantasieland** (open
Apr–Oct daily 9am–6pm; admission fee) is one of Germany's
biggest theme parks. **Schloss Augustusburg** (open Tues–Fri
9am–noon, 1.30–4pm, Sat–Sun 10am–5pm; admission fee)
rivals any of southern Germany's baroque palaces in sheer
sumptuousness, with a truly stunning central staircase and gorgeous interiors which make a fine setting for state receptions.

Karneval in Cologne

The arrival of Lent is greeted in Cologne, the rest of the Rhineland and
other Roman Catholic parts of Germany with an outburst of merrymaking equalled only by Mardi Gras in warmer climes. The fun starts
on the evening of the Thursday before Ash Wednesday, when women
in fancy dress roam the streets, harassing any men foolish enough to
show themselves. The tempo of events reaches a climax the following Monday – *Rosenmontag* – with a monster parade through the
streets. Presiding over the celebrations is His Dottiness the Prince,
attended by a Peasant and a (usually rather masculine) Virgin and
hordes of costumed revellers. By Ash Wednesday the participants are
well prepared for their 40 days of abstinence.

Bonn

Chosen in 1949 as the capital of West Germany, this medium-sized university town keenly felt its loss of status when Berlin became the seat of parliament after reunification in 1990. But Bonn managed to keep some central-government functions and it has an array of museums and other attractions worthy of a far bigger city. It's also the birthplace of Beethoven, and makes much of the connection; the **Beethoven-Haus** (open Apr–Oct Mon–Sat 10am–6pm, Sun 11am–6pm, Nov–Mar Mon–Sat 10am–5pm, Sun 11am–5pm; admission fee) is a worthy shrine for the great composer's many fans, with evocative items like his love letters and ear trumpet. The streets and squares of Bonn's Altstadt contain many charming old buildings, but the dominant edifices are the pastel-coloured baroque Rathaus and the late Romanesque **Münster** (Minster), with its five towers. The government quarter to the south has partly reinvented itself as a conference centre, and here too are the city's modern museums, strung out along the 'Museum Mile'. The **Kunstmuseum** (Art Gallery; open Tues–Sun 10am–6pm; admission fee) is worth visiting for its holdings of works by local Expressionist August Macke, whose career was cut short when he fell in World War I. But a perhaps more compelling attraction is the **Haus der Geschichte der Bundesrepublik Deutschland** (Museum of Contemporary History; open Tues–Sun 9am–7pm). Far more enthralling than its title might suggest, the museum' excellent displays bring to life the story of the two Germanys in the postwar period.

Aachen

Close to the border with the Netherlands and Belgium, Germany's westernmost city was chosen in AD794 by Charlemagne as the capital of the Holy Roman Empire, not least because of his appreciation of the beneficial effects of its thermal springs. Aachen is still a spa town, with superb mod-

Inside the Aachener Dom

ern facilities, while its cathedral, the **Aachener Dom** (open daily 7am–7pm; fee for guided tour) incorporates one of the great monuments of early medieval Europe, the wondrous octagonal chapel built by the emperor and consecrated in 805. Using bronze, stone and marble taken from Roman remains, and graced with a superb 12th-century chandelier, it is still a breathtaking space. The Gothic chancel added later contains Charlemagne's gilded shrine, and also on view is the simple marble-and-wood throne used by emperors during their coronation ceremony. The cathedral treasury is one of the most richly endowed in Europe.

In a deep and winding valley to the south of Aachen are the timber-framed and slate-roofed houses of one of western Germany's prettiest villages. **Monschau** made its living from textiles, and the **Rotes Haus** (Red House; open Easter– Nov Tues–Sun pm only; admission fee) beautifully evokes the family life of a prosperous clothier.

Düsseldorf

A short way down the Rhine from Cologne, and only half the size of its great competitor, the capital of North-Rhine Westphalia has an altogether different character. While Cologne was ruled by its citizenry, Düsseldorf was the seat of the glittering court of the dukes of Berg, and still wears something of an aristocratic air, best exemplified in the ducal **Schloss Benrath** (open mid-Mar–Oct Tues–Sun 10am–6pm, Nov–mid-Mar 11am–5pm; admission fee), a lovely baroque palace set in formal gardens just outside town. Contemporary city glitter is concentrated along the leafy avenue of Königsallee ('Kö' for short), one of Germany's most prestigious shopping thoroughfares, off which are boutique-crammed malls.

Kunstsammlung Nordrhein-Westfalen in Düsseldorf

Much of the wealth produced in the Ruhr has traditionally been spent in Düsseldorf, and not just on shopping; the city's Altstadt has been called 'the longest bar in the world', and is given over almost entirely to pubs, restaurants, nightclubs and other places of entertainment. High culture is not neglected either, with galleries and museums grouped in an 'art axis' running north from the centre. In its modern building, the **Kunstsammlung Nordrhein-Westfalen** (open Tues–Fri 10am–6pm,

Sat–Sun 11am–6pm; admission fee) is known as K20, indicating its devotion to art of the 20th century. Its pride is the collection of over 100 works by Paul Klee. The recently completely reorganised **Museum Kunstpalast** (open Tues–Sun 11am– 6pm, Fri 8pm; admission fee) has German works from medieval times to the present, and includes a superb glass collection. Away from the art axis, in the old *Land* parliament building, and complementing K20, is **K21** (open Tues–Fri 10am–6pm, Sat–Sun 11am–6pm; admission fee), celebrating the art of today.

There are fine views of the Rhine from the Rheinuferpromenade in Düsseldorf's city centre, but the most spectacular panorama is from the 172-m (565-ft) Rheinturm (Rhine Tower; open daily 10am–11.30pm; admission fee), to the south.

The Ruhr

Covering some 5,000 sq km (1,800 sq miles), the vast conurbation of the Ruhrgebiet (Ruhr Area) has lost most of the coal mines and steelworks which made it the industrial powerhouse of Germany, but has valiantly attempted to turn its industrial heritage into visitor attractions. Strung out along a 400-km (250-mile) 'Route Industriekultur', they include Essen's **Zeche Zollverein** (Zollverein Colliery; open Apr–Oct daily 10am–7pm, Nov–Mar daily 10am–5pm; admission fee), Bochum's **Deutsches Bergbaumuseum** (National Mining Museum; open Tues–Fri 8.30am–5pm, Sat–Sun 10am–5pm; admission fee), and the **Eisenbahnmuseum** (Railway

Museum; open Wed, Fri–Sun 10am–5pm; admission fee), also in Bochum, with a large collection of rolling stock and frequent live steam action.

But the Ruhr offers much more. Far from being just a sprawling collection of industrial suburbs, it's a constellation of real cities and lesser towns, all proud of their identity and many with cultural institutions – theatres, opera houses, galleries – of the first order. Essen is a cathedral city, and the **Schatzkammer** (Treasury; open Tues–Sat 10am–5pm, Sun 11.30am–5pm; admission fee) of its Dom is full of fabulous treasures. Away from the centre, the city's museum complex includes an excellent regional museum, the **Ruhrland-museum** (open Tues–Sun 10am–6pm; admission fee), and the **Museum Folkwang** (open Tues–Sun 10am–6pm; admission fee), which has one of the finest collections in the country of 19th- and 20th-century German art. However, Essen's most fascinating offering is the home of its most famous citizen, ironmaster and 'Cannon King', Alfred Krupp. Standing in lovely parkland overlooking the Baldeneysee reservoir, the monstrous **Villa Hügel** (open Tues–Sun 10am–6pm; admission fee) is full of mementos of the dynasty who were friends with both Kaiser and Führer, and who supplied Germany with some of its most destructive weaponry in two world wars.

Münster and the Münsterland

The capital city of the old province of Westphalia is a stately place, its cobbled streets lined with high-gabled town mansions, its formidable Romanesque-cum-Gothic cathedral endowed with a splendid astronomical clock, still in full working order after nearly 500 years. The treaty ending the Thirty Years' War was signed in Münster in 1648; the centre-piece of the **Rathaus** (open Tues–Fri 10am–5pm, Sat–Sun 10am–4pm; admission fee) is the wonderfully panelled Friedenssaal (Hall of Peace) where the ceremony took place.

Burg Vischering in the Münsterland

The flat, damp countryside around the city, the Münsterland, is studded with dozens of moated country houses and castles. Two of the loveliest, Haus Rüschhaus and Burg Hülsoff, are associated with Germany's foremost female poet, Annette von Droste-Hülsoff (1797–1848), but the finest of these so-called *Wasserburgen* is **Burg Vischering** (open Apr–Oct 10am–12.30pm, 1.30–5.30pm, Nov–Mar until 4.30pm; admission fee), a rambling construction in mellow brick and stone built on a pair of islands and housing the Münsterlandmuseum.

Rhine Valley and Mosel Valley

Both Rhine and Mosel have become bywords for a certain kind of tourism, its emblems the smart white pleasure steamer, the robber baron's crag-top castle, and the vineyard clinging to a precipitous slope. The general revelry filling the cobbled streets and wine taverns of one pretty wine village after the other makes its contribution too.

The most glamorous stretch of the **Rhine** begins just upstream from Bonn, where the rounded hills of the **Siebengebirge** (Seven Mountains) include the Drachenfels (Dragon Rock) where heroic Siegfried is said to have slain his fire-breathing adversary.

Overlooked by the huge fortress of Ehrenbreitstein, the town of **Koblenz** stands at the confluence of the Rhine and Mosel. Having risen as the Moselle in the far-off Vosges Mountains of France, the **Mosel** enters Germany near **Trier**, the country's best-preserved Roman city, its symbol the great blackened gateway known as the Porta Nigra. Between here and Koblenz, the river loops in great bends past vineyards which in the past have yielded some of the world's most expensive wines. High points include the picturesque villages of **Bernkastel-Kues** and **Cochem**, as well as the impossibly romantic castle of **Burg Eltz** (open Apr–Oct daily

The Rhine Valley, with the town of Bacharach

9.30am–5.30pm; admission fee), its sheer walls rising through the treetops, its interiors still with their original furnishings.

Immediately to the south of Koblenz, the Rhine emerges from a dramatic, twisting gorge, some 60km (40 miles) long, where the narrowness, speed and depth of the river, as well as the presence of rapids, once made

The Mäuseturm

navigation perilous – to say nothing of the depredations of robber barons. The barons' strongholds are mostly in ruins, but it's possible to visit the most formidable of them all, **Burg Rheinfels** (open Mar–Sept daily 9am–6pm, Oct–Feb Sat–Sun 11am–5pm; admission fee) high above the village of St Goar. Unusual fortifications to look out for are the **Mäuseturm** (Mice Tower) and the **Pfalz**, toll-castles standing four-square in the stream.

All the riverside villages and small towns along the way hope to entice visitors off their boats, none more determinedly than roistering **Rüdesheim** at the southern end of the gorge, with one wine tavern after another lining its famous main street, the Drosselgasse. More dignified places include **Boppard**, an ancient town with remains of its Roman and medieval defences.

The one essential sight along the way, however, is the **Lorelei rock**, from which a fair-haired siren is supposed to have lured sailors to a watery grave with the seductive power of her song. Her story, and much else besides, is recounted in a modern visitor centre, the **Loreley Besucherzentrum** (Apr–Oct daily 10am–5pm; admission fee).

SOUTHWEST TO THE BLACK FOREST

To the south of the dynamic urban region centred on Frankfurt, the Rhine flows through a broad valley bounded by upland massifs. This is one of the sunniest regions of Germany, where vines flourish and, in the smaller places at least, life is lived in a relaxed way. The heat of summer is balanced by the cooler climate of the uplands, among them the Black Forest, which, together with Germany's largest lake, the Bodensee, numbers among the country's favourite holiday areas. Contrasting cities include fan-shaped Karlsruhe, the world-famous old university cities of Heidelberg and Freiburg, and up-to-the-minute Stuttgart.

Frankfurt-am-Main

With its spectacular cluster of skyscrapers, Germany's financial capital on the River Main has earned the nickname 'Bankfurt' or even 'Mainhattan'. Astride strategic communication routes, the city has always gained a good living from commerce, as well as being an important meeting place. For centuries it was here that Germany's rulers came together to elect kings and emperors, many of whom were crowned in the cathedral. In 1848, it was in the city's Paulskirche that delegates from all over Central Europe assembled in an ill-fated attempt to establish a united, democratic Germany. The millions who come here nowadays arrive via converging *Autobahnen*, by high-speed train or through the huge airport, continental Europe's busiest.

As well as being the seat of the Bundesbank, the European Central Bank and the German Stock Exchange, today's Frankfurt is a centre of media and publishing. The *Frankfurter Allgemeine Zeitung* is generally regarded as the country's leading daily paper and the Frankfurt Book Fair is the world's most important event of its kind. Nevertheless, the city retains a rustic

The Römerberg with the Imperial Cathedral

sense of its roots, notably with its devotion to the local drink, *Äppelwoi*, cider made from the orchards all around, best consumed in the taverns of the charming old quarter of Sachsenhausen, just across the river from the sophisticated city centre.

Explorations of Frankfurt usually start at its historical core, the cobbled square known as the **Römerberg**, meticulously reconstructed after being reduced to rubble like most of the city in World War II. Opposite a splendid group of tall timber-framed town mansions is the **Römer**, the old city hall, and here too is the 13th-century red sandstone Nikolaikirche. The **Historisches Museum** (Historical Museum; open Tues, Thur, Fri, Sun 10am–5pm, Wed 10am–8pm, Sat 10am–1pm; admission fee) is worth visiting if only to see poignantly contrasting models of the city before and after its near total destruction. To the east, beyond the controversial postmodern art gallery called the Schirn, stands the 13th-century **Kaiserdom** (Imperial Cathedral; Mon–Thur, Sat 9am–noon, 2.30–

6pm, Fri 2.30–6pm, Sun 2–6pm; free), whose most striking feature is its tower, completed according to the plans of the medieval architect only in 1877. Until the advent of sky-scrapers it was the city's tallest structure. Nearby is another assertive postmodern edifice, the **Museum für Moderne Kunst** (Modern Art Museum; open Tues, Thur–Sun 10am–5pm, Wed 10am–8pm; admission fee), whose emphasis is on late 20th-century European and American art.

The Museum Mile

The majority of Frankfurt's galleries and museums are grouped in the 'museum mile' stretching along the Main embankment opposite the city centre. There are institutions devoted to film, architecture, postal services, ethnography, antique sculpture and the applied arts, but most visitors head first to the **Städelsches Kunstinstitut** (open Tues, Fri–Sun 10am–5pm,

Frankfurt's spectacular cluster of skyscrapers

Wed–Thur 10am–9pm; admission fee). This is one of the country's great picture galleries, with more than 600 masterpieces of European painting from the 14th century onwards. The portrait *Goethe in the Campagna* by Tischbein is one of the gallery's evergreens; Goethe was born in Frankfurt, and many make the pilgrimage to his birthplace, the sensitively restored **Goethe-Haus** (open Mon–Fri, Sun 10am–5.30pm, Sat 10am–6pm; admission fee). Another place of memory is the **Jüdisches Museum** (Jewish Museum: open Tues, Thur–Sun 10am–5pm, Wed 10am–8pm; admission fee), whose displays evoke the long history of Frankfurt's Jewish community, which before the Holocaust was one of Germany's largest.

The Rhine–Main Area

Frankfurt is at the centre of a constellation of prosperous cites and towns with a population of several million, but is also within easy reach of fine countryside. To the west are the sun-soaked vineyards of the Rheingau, and to the south the lovely forested uplands of the Odenwald. To the north are more woods and hills in the Taunus, on the edge of which stands the attractive little spa of **Bad Homburg**. Homburg, which gave its name to a hat, was a favourite resort of Kaiser Wilhelm II, as was the much larger **Wiesbaden**, capital of the *Land* of Hessen. People still come to this elegant town to soak in the thermal waters first enjoyed by the Romans, congregating around the superb domed neo-classical edifice of the Kurhaus, now a casino.

Almost opposite Wiesbaden on the far bank of the Rhine is another capital, **Mainz**, from where the *Land* of Rheinland-Pfalz (Rhineland Palatinate) is governed. Also founded by the Romans, Mainz has long been used to ruling. In the Middle Ages its archbishops were among the most powerful figures in Germany, and many of them lie in splendid state in the nave of the city's six-towered Romanesque **Dom** (open

Mar–Oct Mon–Fri 9am–6.30pm, Sat 9am–4pm, Sun 12.45–3pm, 4–6.30pm; restricted hours in winter; free), a great monument of red sandstone. The city's most famous son was the inventor of printing, Johannes Gutenberg, and the **Gutenberg-Museum** (open Tues–Sat 9am–5pm, Sun 11am–3pm; admission fee) does him justice.

Not a capital of anything any more, but still with a fascinating heritage, the area's other sizeable town, **Darmstadt**, was until 1918 the seat of the grand dukes of Hessen-Darmstadt. Under the patronage of the last duke, a pioneering Art Nouveau artists' colony was established at **Mathildenhöhe** (Matilda's Heights). Many of the original buildings can be seen, including the extraordinary 48-m (157-ft) 'Wedding Tower', while the artists' work is on view in the **Museum Künstlerkolonie** (open Tues–Sun 10am–5pm; admission fee), as well as in the town's principal museum, the **Hessisches Landesmuseum** (open Tues–Sat 10am–5pm, Wed 10am–8pm, Sun 11am–5pm; admission fee).

Heidelberg and Around

Few sights in Germany are quite as romantic as **Heidelberg** and its **castle**, especially when the rambling red sandstone ruin high above the town and the River Neckar is seen bathed in late-afternoon light against a background of glorious wooded hills. This image, together with *Student Prince* memories of roistering, duelling students in fraternity uniforms, brings millions of visitors every year to the undeniably picturesque university town, whose focal point is the cobbled Marktplatz. The square is overlooked by the Heiliggeistkirche (Church of the Holy Spirit), built from the same stone as the castle, but perhaps the most fascinating edifice is the amazingly ornate corner building called the Haus zum Ritter. Not far away is the old Studentenkarzer, the student prison where many an unruly undergraduate was locked up.

Heidelberg's romantic setting

Heidelberg's **schloss** (open daily 8am–5.30pm; admission fee to interior) can be reached by steps or funicular. A wonderful conglomeration of building styles from the 13th to the 17th century, it houses a fascinating pharmaceutical museum as well as the truly gigantic Grosses Fass, a monster barrel filled annually with that portion of the wine harvest compulsorily delivered to the castle.

Upstream from Heidelberg, the steep-sided valley of the winding Neckar is a kind of Rhine gorge in miniature, with vineyards, hilltop strongholds, and attractive villages and old towns. Downstream, the river joins the Rhine at **Mannheim**, a rare example of a large, planned baroque city, with a chequerboard layout of intersecting streets uniquely identified not by names but by letters and numbers. The centrepiece of this grandiose example of town planning, the schloss, remains, but as a forward-looking industrial city the rest of Mannheim has a modern aspect. The past is more alive at nearby **Schwetzingen**, where the **Schlossgarten** (open daily 8am–8pm or dusk) is one of the great gardens of Europe, a mixture of formal and romantic landscape styles, with a number of fantastical garden buildings.

On the far side of the Rhine, the towns of **Worms** and **Speyer** are dominated by their massive cathedrals, splendidly towered edifices which are among the greatest achievements of Romanesque architecture. The Imperial Diet (Assembly) met at Worms, and it was before it that Martin Luther appeared in 1521, uttering his famous words of defiance, 'Here stand I, I can do no other.' To the west, the Rhine plain gives way to the wooded heights of the Pfälzer Wald

Speyer Cathedral

(Palatinate Forest), at whose foot runs the **Deutsche Weinstrasse** (German Wine Route). The well-signposted route passes through one delightful wine village after another, among them **Rhodt**, which has some fine stone and timber-framed vintners' houses, and **Deidesheim**, a famous centre of gastronomy.

Karlsruhe and Stuttgart

A relatively new town, **Karlsruhe** was laid out in the early 18th century by Karl-Wilhelm, the Margrave of Baden, in the form of a fan, with a pattern of streets radiating out from a imposing baroque schloss. The schloss is now the **Badisches Lan-**

desmuseum (Baden Regional Museum; open Tues–Thur 10am–5pm, Fri–Sun 10am–6pm; admission fee). Its fine collections including wonderful trophies from the Turkish wars. The geometrical layout of the city can be appreciated from the top of the tower. Most of Karlsruhe's 18th-century buildings have gone, but there are some fine neo-classical st-

Staatsgalerie in Stuttgart

ructures around the central Marktplatz, at its centre a strange sandstone pyramid marking Karl-Wilhelm's tomb.

Stuttgart was the capital of the kingdom of Württemberg up until 1918, and is now capital of the *Land* of Baden-Württemberg. Today's Stuttgart shows only a few signs of its regal past, being a resolutely modern city with an identity based on its scientific and technological achievements. It was in Stuttgart in 1883 that Gottlob Daimler patented the internal combustion engine, and today the city is home to Mercedes and Porsche, as well as other manufacturing companies. The **Mercedes Museum** is well worth a visit, as is the smaller establishment devoted to the products of the Porsche works. The old royal schloss is now the **Landesmuseum** (Regional Museum; open Wed–Sun 10am–5pm, Tues 10am–1pm; admission fee), whose star exhibit is the Württemberg crown jewels. But Stuttgart's most high-profile museum is the **Staatsgalerie** (open Tues–Sun 10am–6pm, Thur until 9pm; admission fee). This is one of the country's finest art collections, with a particular emphasis on early 20th-century German artists, whose works are housed in a stunning postmodern extension by the British architect James Stirling.

A clearing in the Black Forest

Black Forest

➤ The best-known of all Germany's upland massifs, the **Black Forest** or **Schwarzwald** extends for about 160km (100 miles) southwards from Karlsruhe to the Swiss border. Its blackness is attributed to its dark forests of spruce and fir, but as well as woodland there are mountain pastures, rushing streams and crashing waterfalls, magnificent timber farm-houses and living folkways. The highest point of the Black Forest is the **Feldberg** at 1,493m (4,898ft), a flattened mountain whose summit can be easily reached from the car park. On clear days the view extends to the far-away Bernese Alps. A drive along the scenic route called the Schwarzwald-Hochstrasse is one way of getting to know the area, but the Black Forest is best explored on foot from any one of the numerous highland resorts. The most popular resort is the invariably crowded **Titisee**, beautifully sited on the lake of the same name, but there are many other places to stay. Satisfying one's natural curiosity about Black Forest cuckoo clocks – and about timepieces of all kinds – can be done at the excellent **Deutsches Uhrenmuseum** (National Clock Museum; open Apr–Oct daily 9am–6pm, Nov–Mar daily 10am–5pm; admission fee). The area's distinctive building heritage can be seen everywhere, and in concentrated form at the **Schwarzwälder Freilichtmuseum** (Black Forest Open-air Museum; open late Mar–early Nov daily 9am–6pm; admission fee), where traditional farming techniques are also demonstrated.

The Black Forest's western edge drops abruptly to the broad plain of the Rhine. One of the best panoramas is from the 1,284-m (4,213-ft) high **Schauinsland** viewpoint, reached by cable car from the ancient cathedral and university city of **Freiburg**. Overlooked by the tall spire of its superb Gothic **Münster** (Minster), Freiburg is a well-preserved town, with a wealth of old buildings, museums, and places to eat and be entertained. Its relaxed lifestyle may have something to do with the vineyards clothing the lower slopes of the Black Forest and the nearby Kaiserstuhl (Emperor's Seat), an ancient volcano sticking up out of the plain. When

Black Forest Cuckoo Clocks

That enduring symbol of the Black Forest, the cuckoo clock, has a fascinating history going back to the 17th century. This was a time of agricultural depression, and farmers used to handling wood looked for alternative ways of making a living. Clockmaking as a cottage industry soon took off and, by the 19th century, beautifully carved Black Forest clocks were being exported all over the world. It was around this time that the cuckoo made its appearance, to become a firm, if sometimes irritating, favourite. Clockmaking declined in the late 20th century, but has since revived.

strolling around, visitors should watch out for the town's *Bächle*, narrow water channels threading through the streets.

Frieburg is a useful gateway to the Black Forest, as is **Baden-Baden**, the queen of all spa towns. Set in a lovely wooded valley, the town's springs were discovered by the Romans, and one of the spas – with state-of-the-art buildings and facilities – is named after the Emperor Caracalla who spent time here. Baden-Baden's heyday was in the late 19th century, when it was known as the 'Summer Capital of Europe', attracting the continent's royalty and aristocracy and their hangers-on. The town has succeeded in keeping much of the allure of that golden age, with an opulent casino and immaculately maintained parks and gardens.

Lake Constance

To the east of the Black Forest there's plenty of fine country-side, albeit not quite on the same grand scale. Attractive small towns abound, too, none prettier than the medieval university city of **Tübingen**, where students punt along the river. With its medieval walls and towers intact, **Rottweil** is also worth a detour. But most visitors passing this way are heading south to **Lake Constance** (Bodensee in German), the great body of water shared with Austria and Switzerland and bounded to the south by the Alps. Fed by the Rhine, the lake enjoys a balmy climate and, lined with orchards and vineyards as well as fascinating towns and villages, is an ideal holiday destination, understandably busy in summer. The area's largest town, **Konstanz**, stands astride the Rhine as it flows out of the main lake, the Übersee, into the lower lake, the Untersee. The town's great moment of glory came when it hosted the Council of Konstanz in 1414–18, now chiefly remembered for the burning at the stake of the radical Czech clergyman, Jan Hus. Spared by Allied bombers because of its proximity to the Swiss border, Konstanz is a pleasure to stroll around.

Lake Constance at Lindau

The same is true of the little island city of **Lindau**, on the lake's northeastern corner. Reached by causeway from the mainland, Lindau has fine old patrician houses and a lovely harbour looking over the lake to the mountains. Other delightful old towns on this sunny, southwest-facing shore include **Meersburg** and **Überlingen**, while more workaday **Friedrichshafen** – former home of the Zeppelin company – boasts the **Zeppelinmuseum** (open May–Oct Tues–Sun 9am–5pm, Nov–Apr Tues–Sun 10am–5pm; admission fee), whose prize exhibit is a superb full-size recreation of the passenger deck of the ill-fated *Hindenburg* airship.

The lake's islands include tranquil **Reichenau**, with a set of remarkable Romanesque monastery churches, and ever-popular **Mainau** (open daily 7am–8pm or until sunset; admission fee), a paradise of sub-tropical luxuriance, with terraced gardens rising from the lakeshore to a baroque schloss and church.

Gemütlichkeit in a Munich beer garden

MUNICH AND THE SOUTH

Southern Bavaria is perhaps the most glamorous part of Germany, and certainly the most popular part of the country for holidaymakers, with villages of timber houses clustering round onion-domed churches against an Alpine background of lakes, forests and high peaks. This is where 'Mad King' Ludwig sited his impossibly romantic castles, and the visitor is frequently reminded that Bavaria was a kingdom almost within living memory. Even today, it is proud to be not just a run-of-the-mill *Land*, but *Freistaat Bayern* (the Free State of Bavaria), with a right royal capital, Munich.

➤ Munich

The Bavarian metropolis magically combines a forward-looking, cosmopolitan character with a folksy, small-town atmosphere where people can sometimes still be seen unself-consciously wearing *lederhosen* and *dirndl*, and swaying to the blast of an oompah band while swigging beer from a substantial *stein*. Within sight of the Alps, and with an array of world-class museums and galleries and superb parks, Munich attracts not only visitors from all over the world but also would-be residents from the whole of Germany. The fortunate among them find employment in famous-name, advanced industries like Siemens or BMW, the Bavarian Motor Works.

An old city, founded in the 10th century by monks – who gave it its name and are the origin of its coat of arms, which depicts a monk – Munich rose to prominence when the Wittelsbach dynasty made it the capital of Bavaria in the early 16th century. Much of the city's present regal character can be attributed to them, particularly to King Ludwig I, whose rule lasted from 1825 to 1848. Less famous than a later Ludwig, the 'Mad King', this enlightened monarch was a generous patron of the arts, a founder of museums and galleries, and an ambitious town planner. The last Wittelsbach, Ludwig III, left his ancestors' palatial Residenz in the heart of the city as Marxist revolution broke out in November 1918. A few years later, in 1923, it was in Munich that Adolf Hitler instigated the failed 'Beer Hall Putsch', and his Nazis always considered the city to be the 'capital of the movement'. Badly battered in World War II, Munich rose from the ashes and then used the 1972 Olympics to further modernise and beautify itself, with exemplary public transport facilities, the wholesale pedestrianisation of the city centre, and the creation of the Olympiapark with its futuristic buildings.

The towers of the Frauenkirche

Around Marienplatz

Sooner or later all visitors to Munich finds themselves in this spacious square at the centre of the Altstadt. It is named after the gilded statue of the Virgin Mary atop a column, placed there in 1638 in thanks for the safe deliverance of the city in the Thirty Years' War. The north side of the square is occupied by the exuberant mock-Gothic **Neues Rathaus** (New City Hall), which has a glockenspiel that plays at 11am, noon and 3pm. The old, authentically Gothic city hall to the east now houses a toy museum. There's a fine view from the tower of the new city hall, reached by lift, and another from the tower of the nearby Peterskirche, reached by 300-plus steps.

Neues Rathaus

In the network of streets between Marienplatz and the Residenz is the mother of all beer halls, the **Hofbräuhaus**. Established by ducal decree in the 16th century to supply the court, the 'Court Brewery' is a favourite with visitors from abroad, though there are usually plenty of bewhiskered locals here too, downing beer to the sound of the brass band.

From the Marienplatz, Munich's main traffic-free artery, the Kaufingerstrasse (later called Neuhauserstrasse), runs westwards towards the Karlstor, one of the surviving city gateways. Over the rooftops to the north can be glimpsed the twin towers and onion domes of Munich's brick-built cathedral, the Gothic **Frauenkirche** (Church of Our Lady), with its simple but wonderfully spacious interior. In the crypt are the tombs of the Wittelsbachs.

Hofbräuhaus sign

Marienplatz was once the site of the city market, but this long outgrew its original location and moved to the **Viktualienmarkt**, a lively place with an amazing array of fruit and vegetables and much else besides, including great places in which to have a snack or a drink. The best place to delve into the history of Munich is in the nearby **Münchner Stadtmuseum**

Oktoberfest

Beer is more than drinkable all over Germany, nowhere more so than in Bavaria and in its capital Munich, home of the archetypal beer hall and of one of Europe's great popular festivals, the Oktoberfest. A fortnight's orgy of eating and drinking, this has its origin in the celebrations accompanying the wedding of King Ludwig I to Princess Theresa in 1810. These took place on the great meadow subsequently named after her, the Theresienwiese, the scene of today's festivities, where enormous tents are erected to shelter the countless revellers and the brass bands entertaining them. The raucous jollity is not to everyone's taste, but no one should miss the huge and colourful procession that winds its way through the city on the day the Oktoberfest begins.

(City Museum; open Tues–Sun 10am–6pm; admission fee), which also features superb collections of musical instruments and puppetry.

Residenz and Englischer Garten

Over the centuries, the rulers of Bavaria transformed what had been a simple moated medieval castle into a sumptuous palace laid out around seven courtyards. The **Residenz** is one of the great treasure houses of Europe, reflecting Wittelsbach wealth, the family's taste as passionate collectors, and their ability to employ the best talents of the time. Too extensive to take in at one go, the state rooms of what is now the Munich **Residenzmuseum** (open Apr–mid-Oct daily 9am–6pm, until 8pm Wed, mid-Oct–Mar daily 10am–4pm; admission fee) can only be seen in their entirety in the course of two guided tours. As well as living quarters re-

The Antiquarium inside the Residenz

flecting the personal prefer-
ences of successive rulers,
there are stunning setpieces
like the rococo Ahnengalerie
(Ancestral Gallery) with its
portraits of Wittelsbach ancestors, the Renaissance Antiquarium, built to house a
collection of antique sculpture and decorated with mu-

> **The ornate Cuvilliés
> Theater was built in
> the mid-18th century
> by François Cuvillié,
> court dwarf and gifted
> designer. It saw the
> premiere in 1781
> of Mozart's opera
> *Idomeneo*.**

rals of Bavarian scenes, and the Kaisersaal (Imperial Hall), a
sumptuous setting for state occasions. One part of the complex not to be missed is the **Cuvilliés Theater** (same opening
times; admission fee), a jewel-like baroque auditorium. Another is the **Schatzkammer** (Treasury; same opening times;
admission fee), one of the most important of its kind, with superb examples of workmanship in gold, silver and precious
stones from around AD1000 to the 19th century.

Part of the Residenz fronts on to the Odeonsplatz,
dominated by the mustard-yellow **Theatinerkirche**, one of
the city's finest examples of baroque church architecture,
and by the Italian-style loggia known as the **Feldherren-
halle** (Commanders' Hall). Built in 1844 to celebrate the
achievements of the Bavarian army, the hall was the focal
point of Hitler's abortive putsch of 1923, and subsequently
became a place of Nazi pilgrimage. North of here stretches
Ludwigstrasse, named after Ludwig I, the monarch responsible for the elegant architectural character of much of this
part of the city. The broad roadway leads to the university
and the vibrant Schwabing district, and terminates at the
triumphal arch of the Siegestor. The popularity of this part of
Munich is partly due to the proximity of the **Englischer
Garten**, one of the largest public parks in the world. Extending 3km (2 miles) north from the formal Hofgarten (Court

Chinese Tower beer garden in the English Garden

Garden) attached to the Residenz, and threaded by rushing sub-Alpine streams, the English Garden has a wealth of features including a Japanese garden, a rotunda with a lovely view of the city skyline, a Chinese tower with a 7,000-seater beer garden, and sweeping lawns for all kinds of activity and inactivity (such as nude sunbathing).

The Museum Quarter

The district to the west of the Ludwigstrasse is one of the world's largest and most richly endowed concentrations of art museums and galleries. The initial impulse was given by Ludwig I, when he ordered the construction of a group of neo-classical edifices around the spacious **Königsplatz**. They include the **Glyptothek** (open Tues, Wed, Fri–Sun 10am–5pm, Thur 10am–8pm; admission fee), which houses a superlative collection of Greek and Roman sculpture; the **Staatliche Antikensammlungen** (State Collections of Antiquities; same opening times; admission fee), an equally magnificent array of bronzes, vases, ceramics and jewellery; and the **Propyläen**, an imposing copy of the gateway guarding the approach to the Acropolis in Athens.

Here too is the **Städtische Galerie im Lenbachhaus** (City Gallery in the Lenbach House; open Tues–Sun 10am–6pm; admission fee), an Italianate villa with a garden to match. Once the home of the portraitist Franz von Lenbach, the gallery is devoted to Munich painting from the 18th century onwards, with particular emphasis on the vibrant, colourful work of the early 20th-century Blauer Reiter group of artists led by Wassily Kandinsky.

But the centre of gravity of the museum area is formed by the trio of prestigious *Pinakotheken* (picture galleries), just to the north. In its 19th-century Venetian-style palace, the **Alte Pinakothek** (Old Picture Gallery; open Tues 10am–8pm, Wed–Sun 10am–5pm; admission fee, but free Sun) is one of the world's finest galleries of European art from the Middle Ages to the 18th century, based on the collections assembled by the Wittelsbachs. Comprehensive in scope, it has works by most of the Old Masters, with a natural emphasis on the German greats like Dürer, Cranach, Grünewald and Altdorfer, whose stunning *Battle of Alexander* of 1529 is one of the most vivid battle scenes of all time.

Albrecht Dürer's *Self-portrait with a Fur Coat*, Alte Pinakothek

The **Neue Pinakothek** (New Picture Gallery; open Wed 10am–8pm, Thur–Mon 10am–5pm; admission fee, but free Sun) is housed in an impressive postmodern edifice (built 1981) nicknamed the Palazzo Branca after its architect Alexander von Branca. Its theme is European painting and sculpture between the 18th and early 20th centuries. Again, German art features strongly, with fine pictures by Romantic artists like Caspar David Friedrich, amusing 19th-century genre scenes by Carl Spitzweg, and works by local equivalents of the French Impressionists such as Lovis Corinth and Max Liebermann. The latter make fascinating comparisons possible with pictures by the likes of Manet and Van Gogh.

The most recent of the trio of *Pinakotheken*, opened in 2002, is the **Pinakothek der Moderne** (Modern Picture Gallery; open Tues–Wed, Sat–Sun 10am–5pm, Thur–Fri 10am–8pm; admission fee, but free Sun). This elegant edifice contains four galleries. The Bavarian State Gallery of Modern Art has a superb collection of 20th- and 21st-century work, ranging from German Expressionism and European Surrealism to American Abstract Expressionism and Pop Art. A whole room is devoted to Picasso. The Neue Sammlung presents what is claimed to be one of the most comprehensive collections of design objects anywhere, ranging from car design to computers. The Graphische Sammlung has more than 400,000 drawings and prints, and the Architekturmuseum an astonishing array of architectural drawings and models.

A Junkers aircraft in the Deutsches Museum

Deutsches Museum

The largest of Munich's museums is not in the museum quarter but on its own island in the River Isar. The **Deutsches Museum** (open daily 9am–5pm; admission fee) is one of the world's leading museums of science and technology and Germany's most popular attraction of its kind. In dozens of sections spread over six floors there are countless exhibits, inviting interactive experiences, and compelling live demonstrations. It is possible to concentrate in depth on a particular subject or simply to wander throughout the huge building wondering at the beauty and fascination of the objects on display, among them historic aircraft, locomotives, boats and road vehicles. As well as a planetarium, there are realistic recreations of a coal mine and of the prehistoric cave paintings of Altamira in Spain.

Olympiapark

Olympiapark

Few Olympic host cities have built on so lavish a scale as Munich did in 1972, when an old airfield in the northern part of the city was transformed into a world-class set of sports facilities. The park features a range of subtly contoured artificial hills, while the 290-m (950-ft) Olympia Tower offers incomparable views over Munich towards the Alps. Very much in use today, the great event hall, the stadium and the swimming pool are still covered by an innovative tent-like roof structure. Munich has built an equally innovative edifice to host some of the events of the 2006 football World Cup. Nicknamed the UFO, the cigar-shaped 60,000-seater Allianz-Arena on the northern outskirts is clad in a spectacular translucent skin with the startling ability to glow in different colours.

Nymphenburg

On Munich's western outskirts, the Wittelsbach's sumptuous baroque summer palace, **Schloss Nymphenburg** (open Apr–Sept daily 9am–6pm, Oct–Mar daily 10am–4pm; admission fee) was begun in the mid-17th century and largely completed in the mid-18th. Its most splendid interior is the Steinerner Saal, while in the south wing is Ludwig I's Schönheitsgalerie (Gallery of Beauties), his famous collection of female portraits. The palace stables house an array of fabulously ornate royal coaches and sleighs, while the floor above is devoted to the products of the renowned Nymphenburg porcelain factory. The vast park is a wonderful fusion of French and English landscape styles, with pavilions rivalling the palace in their elaborate architecture and decor.

Neuschwanstein and Other Royal Castles

The fantastical castles and palaces built by King Ludwig II may have bankrupted his kingdom, but they proved to be a wise long-term investment, having become some of Germany's most visited tourist attractions. Foremost among them is the almost impossibly romantic **Schloss Neuschwanstein** (open Apr–Sept daily 8am–6pm, Oct–Mar daily 9am–4pm;

'Mad King' Ludwig

Prince Otto Ludwig Friedrich Wilhelm ascended the Bavarian throne in 1864. It soon became evident that he preferred fantasy to reality, turning away from state duties to live in a world inspired by Wagner's operas and indulge in a fascination with the extravagant culture of 18th-century France. In 1886, with his ever more ambitious building projects draining the state coffers, he was deposed and declared insane. Within days, together with his personal psychiatrist, he was found drowned in the Starnberger See, a lake south of Munich.

admission fee; timed tours), perched high up on a crag above a gorge. Begun in 1869, it's a vision of what the Middle Ages might have been, and was inspired by Ludwig's musical mentor, Richard Wagner (its interiors are filled with references to Wagner's operas). Some of the castle's interiors, like the Minstrel's Hall and the Throne Room, are decorated with the utmost extravagance, but the castle was never completed, and the unfortunate Ludwig spent little time here. The best view of Schloss Neuschwanstein in its wild setting is from the little bridge high above, the Marienbrücke.

At the foot of Neuschwanstein is the much older **Schloss Hohenschwangau** (same opening times; admission fee), a Wittelsbach summer residence where Ludwig spent a happy childhood.

Neuschwanstein Castle

Set deep among the Ammergebirge Alps to the east of Neuschwanstein, **Schloss Linderhof** (open Apr–Oct daily 9am–6pm, Nov–Mar daily 10am–4pm; admission fee) is perhaps the most appealing of Ludwig's creations, an elegant white villa standing on the mountainside among lovely terraced gardens.

The 'mad king's' most expensive project was built on an island in Bavaria's biggest lake, Chiemsee, to the southeast of Munich. **Schloss Herrenchiemsee** (open mid-Mar–late Sept daily 9am–6pm, late Sept–mid-Mar daily 9.40am–4.15pm; admission fee) was modelled on Versailles, even including a 100m (30ft) Hall of Mirrors, but like Neuschwanstein was left unfinished. Among the attractions here is a fascinating museum devoted to Ludwig.

Garmisch-Partenkirchen

Germany's glamorous winter sports centre at the foot of the country's highest peak, the **Zugspitze** (2,962m/9,718ft), is also much in vogue for summer holidays, with endless opportunities for walkers and climbers in the glorious country all around. Partenkirchen is the older of the two merged towns, its main street lined with colourfully painted houses. Garmisch has a picturesque old quarter too, but its centre is more characterised by sophisticated shops and boutiques. From here it is easy to get to **Oberammergau**, renowned not only for its Passion Play, staged every 10 years, but also for its incredibly skilled woodcarvers and for the art of *luftlmalerei*, the 'paintings in the air' that adorn many of the house facades. It's also easy to ascend the Zugspitze, by cable car or rack railway. A clear day attracts a capacity crowd to gaze in awe at the amazing views over much of the Alps.

Traditional architecture in Garmisch

Berchtesgaden

Once a favourite summer retreat of the Bavarian royal family, the delightful small town of **Berchtesgaden** and its surroundings encapsulate all the attractions of the Bavarian Alps. Painted houses, a

Königsee, St Bartolomä and the East Face of the Watzmann

little royal palace and wonderful views contribute to the allure of the town, which is also the home of the **Nationalpark-Haus** , the interpretive centre for the national park which protects the area's sublime but vulnerable landscape. The town's ancient prosperity depended on salt, and visitors can enjoy a thrilling trip into the depths of the old salt mines, the **Salzbergwerk**. Another trip is up the mountain road to the 'Eagle's Nest', Hitler's perch atop the 1,834-m (6,017-ft) **Kehlstein**, now a panoramic restaurant. Near the foot of the mountain is the **Dokumentation Obersalzberg**, an information centre documenting the area's Third Reich connections. But the essential excursion hereabouts is aboard one of the electrically powered boats which glide across the crystal-clear waters of the **Königsee**, giving views of Germany's second-highest mountain, the Watzmann (2,713m/8,900ft), and tying up along the much-photographed onion-domed church of St Bartolomä.

Augsburg and Ulm

Two small cities to the west of Munich reward exploration. Founded in 15BC and named after Emperor Augustus, **Augsburg**, 80km (50 miles) away, had its heyday in the late Middle Ages, when the Fugger family made it Central Europe's banking centre. Their **Fuggerei**, a gated complex of old people's homes, was the first of its kind in the world, and is still home to deserving pensioners. With streets and squares beautified by Renaissance fountains and lined with fine patrician houses, Augsburg is a stately city, its pride and wealth on ostentatious display in the Golden Hall of the Rathaus and in the sumptuous furnishings and fittings of the cathedral.

Ulm lies just over the Bavarian border in the *Land* of Baden-Württemberg, 80km (50 miles) west of Augsburg. The city's pride is its **Münster** (Minster), which boasts the world's tallest spire (161m/525ft), as well as an array of superb artworks in its interior. Ulm's grand Gothic and Renaissance Rathaus contrasts with the tumbledown buildings of the picturesque riverside **Fischer-Viertel** (Fishermen's Quarter), best viewed from the ramparts.

Landshut and Passau

Some 75km (46 miles) northeast of Munich, the old provincial capital of **Landshut**, once the seat of a branch of the Wittelsbach family, has kept much of its medieval atmosphere, with gabled and arcaded mansions lining the main street. The town is overlooked by the ducal castle high above, and by the cathedral tower, built in brick and the tallest of its kind anywhere. This well-preserved townscape forms a fine background to the four-yearly *Fürstenhochzeit*, a lavish re-enactment of the wedding in 1475 of the then duke to a Polish princess.

On a tongue of land at the confluence of three rivers, the Danube, Inn and Ilz, just upstream from the frontier with Austria, **Passau** has perhaps the most distinctive setting of any German city. Keeping a watchful eye on the town from the wooded heights above is **Veste Oberhaus**, the fortress built by the city's prince-bishops, now the regional museum. Passau's pretty painted houses are arranged around the bishops' downtown Residenz, the tall-towered Rathaus and the cathedral, which contains the world's largest organ.

Regensburg and Around

As one of the country's largest cities to have remained unscathed by war, **Regensburg**, 130km (80 miles) north of Munich, has a full roster of historical delights to offer the visitor. Founded by the Romans to guard their frontier on the Danube, in the Middle Ages it was the biggest city in Bavaria, and has kept a wealth of ancient buildings lining the grid pattern of streets and alleyways established by the Romans. Unique in Germany are the fortified tower houses built by

Regensburg's medieval Steinerne Brücke (Stone Bridge)

prosperous medieval merchant families to flaunt their wealth and status; some 30 of these extraordinary structures have survived. Another remarkable survivor is the **Steinerne Brücke** (Stone Bridge), a 15-span marvel of medieval engineering thrown across the Danube in the mid-12th century. From it there is a fine prospect of the city still looking much as it must have done in the Middle Ages; beyond the gateway and clock tower guarding the bridge approach rises Regensburg's cathedral, the finest Gothic structure in Bavaria, begun in the 13th century and completed in the 19th with the addition of delicate openwork spires. Its sculpture of the 'Laughing Angel' is famous, as is its array of stained glass. The city's most illustrious family was the princely dynasty of Thurn and Taxis, pioneers in the 16th century of reliable postal services. The opulent lifestyle they enjoyed is on show in the **Schloss Thurn und Taxis** (open for guided tour only Apr–Oct daily 11am, 2pm, 3pm, 4pm; Nov–Mar Sat–Sun 10am, 11am, 2pm, 3pm; admission fee). The tour also takes in lovely medieval cloisters.

High above the Danube a short distance downstream from Regensburg stands the gleaming white neo-Grecian temple of **Walhalla** (open daily Apr–Sept 9am–5.45pm, Oct daily 9am–4.45pm, Nov–Mar daily 10am–11.45am, 1–3.45pm; admission fee), built by King Ludwig I of Bavaria in 1842 to honour Germany's heroes. Conceived in the heady days of German nationalism, its array of more than 120 busts begins with the 10th-century King Henry the Fowler, and it is still being added to; the lat-

Glassblower in the Bavarian Forest

est to be honoured is Sophie Scholl, the Munich student executed by the Nazis for her resistance to the regime.

At Kelheim, some 32km (20 miles) upstream from Regensburg, another prominent 19th-century monument overlooks the confluence of the Danube and the Altmühl rivers. The circular **Befreiungshalle** (Hall of Liberation) commemorates the German victory over Napoleon in 1813. Beyond Kelheim the River Danube flows through a spectacular limestone gorge, a fine location for the monastery of **Weltenburg**; its church is one of the most gloriously theatrical

The dense Bavarian Forest

examples of baroque architecture in Bavaria. Limestone cliffs fringe stretches of the Altmühl valley, an area of tranquil countryside, much of it protected as a nature park. The 'capital' of the valley is the exquisite little episcopal town of **Eichstätt** with a cathedral and pastel-coloured rococo residences.

Almost unknown to visitors from abroad, but much loved by German holidaymakers, the vast Bavarian Forest along the border with the Czech Republic has been called 'Europe's Green Roof'. Dense conifer woodland clads much of the area, which rises to 1,456m (4,777ft) at the bleak summit of the **Grosser Arber**, reached by chairlift. Part of the forest is a designated national park, its flora and fauna expertly explained in the **Hans-Eisenmann-Haus** visitor centre near Neuschönau.

NUREMBERG AND NORTHERN BAVARIA

Only incorporated into Bavaria in relatively recent times, this part of the country seems to encapsulate much of the essence of Germany. Here are beautifully preserved or immaculately rebuilt historic cities, ranging in size from old provincial capitals like Nuremberg and Würzburg to exquisite small towns like Rothenburg-ob-der-Tauber, Nördlingen and Dinkelsbühl strung out along the country's most popular holiday route, the Romantic Road.

➤ Nuremberg

Lovingly rebuilt after wartime devastation, Nuremberg's Altstadt conveys the atmosphere of the archetypal German medieval city, with formidable defensive walls, streets lined with red-roofed old buildings, squares presided over by great Gothic churches and fabulous fountains. Overlooking it all from rocky height is an Imperial castle. The unchallenged capital of northern Bavaria, Nuremberg is associated not just with emperors and Wagner's Mastersingers, but also with some of the grimmer aspects of Nazism, in particular the ostentatious pageantry of party rallies and the postwar trials of the leaders of the Third Reich.

The Altstadt is divided into roughly equal halves by the River Pegnitz, which is spanned by the picturesque Heilig-Geist-Spital, a 15th-century almshouse. To the south, the twin-towered **Lorenzkirche** contains masterworks by the great craftsmen the city nutured at its zenith in the 15th and early 16th centuries, as does the lovely **Frauenkirche** to the north. The Frauenkirche also has a glockenspiel with performing automata, while the marketplace it stands in is the scene of the Christkindlmarkt, Germany's world-famous Christmas market. Here too is the 19-m (62-ft) Gothic **Schöner Brunnen**, the city's foremost fountain with its astonishing array of statuary.

From here, Burgstrasse leads upwards past the Sebaldskirche and Rathaus to the **Kaiserburg** (Imperial Castle; open Apr–Sept daily 9am–6pm, Oct–Mar daily 10am–4pm; admission fee), a complex structure begun in the 12th century by Emperor Frederick Barbarossa. From the main tower there is a fine panorama over the Altstadt, its roofs pierced by row upon row of dormer windows. Below the castle is the **Albrecht-Dürer-Haus**, the residence of Nuremberg's most famous son. Some of the artist's finest work can be seen in the enormous **Germanisches Nationalmuseum** (open Tues, Thur–Sun 10am–6pm, Wed until 9pm; admission fee), whose huge collection of artefacts spans German culture from the earliest time.

Just beyond the city walls, the **Verkehrsmuseum** (Transport Museum; open Tues–Sun 9am–5pm; admission fee) is the largest of its kind in Germany, with a fine collection of railway artefacts and a huge model railway. Southeast of the

Inside the Verkehrsmuseum in Nuremberg

centre, some of the monster structures erected for the Nazi Party rallies still stand, notably the incomplete congress centre modelled on Rome's Colosseum. Part of it now houses a documentation centre chronicling the Third Reich and Nuremberg's role in it.

Franconia

To the north of Nuremberg, **Fränkische Schweiz** (Franconian Switzerland) is a limestone plateau cut by deep, wooded valleys. The principal town, **Bayreuth**, dates to the 12th century, but its worldwide fame is a relatively modern phenomenon, thanks to the annual opera festival celebrating Richard Wagner and his works. Bayreuth's operatic tradition had begun in the 18th century with the building of a splendid baroque opera house, one of the finest to have survived.

The great jewel of Franconia, however, is perfectly preserved **Bamberg**, divided into the lower citizens' town astride the River Regnitz and the upper bishops' town. The symbol of the former is the extravagantly picturesque, medieval-cum-baroque **Altes Rathaus** (Old Town Hall), perched on an island in the river, the symbol of the latter the glorious four-towered **Dom**, a wonderfully harmonious edifice built as the Romanesque style morphed into Gothic. As well as the splendid tomb of Emperor Heinrich, it contains the enigmatic mounted sculpture known as the Bamberger

The lovely valley of the River Main to the north of Bamberg is flanked by two of Germany's finest 18th-century churches; Kloster Banz to the west, Vierzehnheiligen to the east. Drawing pilgrims in their thousands, Vierzehnheiligen (Church of the Fourteen Saints; open daily 6am–6.30pm, donation requested) was built in the most extravagant rococo style imaginable at the site of a humble shepherd's vision.

Reiter (Bamberg Rider), for long considered to represent the very essence of medieval chivalry, though his identity remains unknown.

Almost on the border with Thuringia, **Coburg** is overlooked from a great height by the old fortress known as the 'Crown of Franconia'. Through judicious intermarriage, the ducal rulers of Coburg spread their genes throughout royal Europe; Queen Victoria's husband, Prince Albert, was born here, and the widowed monarch visited Coburg several times after her consort's death, no doubt reassured by the English Tudor appearance of the ducal schloss. Albert and Victoria were first cousins.

The Bamberger Reiter

Würzburg and the Romantic Road

Among the gesticulating baroque statues gracing the ancient bridge over the River Main at the university city of **Würzburg** is one of St Kilian, an Irish missionary martyred here in the 7th century. A millennium or so later, the Christian ruler here, Prince-Bishop Schönborn, was living in lavish style in the magnificent **Residenz** (open Apr–Oct daily 9am–6pm, Nov–Mar daily 10am–4pm; admission fee) built for him by the architect Balthasar Neumann. This is one of the largest and most flamboyant baroque palaces in Germany, boasting a succession of magnificent interiors and, crowning the huge staircase, the

St Kilian in Würzburg

largest ceiling painting in the world, the work of the Venetian artist Tiepolo. At the centre of the Franconian vineyards, Würzburg has a relaxed atmosphere. There's a winery in the late-medieval hospice known as the Julius-spital, and a tour of the wine-villages along the Main is highly recommended, as is a visit to the prince-bishops' baroque summer palace at **Veitshöchheim** (garden open daily dawn–dusk), 7km (4 miles) from Würzburg. This is the country's most famous rococo garden, its grounds decorated by more than 200 statues.

Würzburg is the starting point of the 350-km (220-mile) **Romantic Road** (*Romantische Strasse*), a signposted holiday route which leads southwards through tranquil countryside and a succession of historic towns to the foot of the Alps. The one essential stop along the way is **Rothenburg-ob-der-Tauber**, its quaint name matching the little medieval city's perfect state of preservation. By blanking out the crowds of visitors wandering the streets, relaxing in the main square, or filing along the sentry-walk running the whole length of the 2.5-km (1½-mile) fortifications, it's easy to imagine oneself transported magically back into an idealised Germany of the Middle Ages. There's a wonderful overall view from the tall tower of the Renaissance Rathaus over Rothenburg's red-tiled rooftops to the lovely Franconian countryside. A stroll around the streets reveals an almost endless succession of delightful townscapes, none more pho-

tographed than the Plönlein, a cobbled space of changing
levels framed by towers and timber-framed houses. Rothenburg was spared from destruction in the Thirty Years' War
when its burgomaster successfully downed a 3.25-litre
(nearly 6-pint) draught of wine, a seemingly impossible feat
re-created each year at the *Meistertrunk* festival.

Almost Rothenburg's equal in picturesqueness, with intact
defences, superb patrician houses and a fine parish church,
Dinkelsbühl escaped a similar fate when its children
appealed en masse to a besieging general. The event is re-
created at the annual *Kinderzeche* festival. **Nördlingen**, too,
has kept its ramparts with their 16 towers and five gateways,
and has an additional, unique attraction in the modern
Rieskrater-Museum, devoted to explaining the story of the
nearby 25-km (16-mile) diameter crater formed by a giant
meteorite 15 million years ago.

Quintessential Romantic Road: Rothenburg-ob-der-Tauber

WHAT TO DO

With a coast, mountains, rivers and lakes, and a great variety of landscapes, Germany caters for most types of outdoor activity, and facilities are generally of excellent quality. For further information about sporting activities, see the German National Tourist Office's website <www.germany-tourism.de> or those of the bodies listed below (note that not all sites are in English).

ACTIVE PURSUITS

Hiking and cycling. Germany has a large and well-signposted network of footpaths, particularly well developed in the mountains and nature parks. Cyclists are also well catered for, both in towns and in rural areas, and it is easy to find bikes for hire. Long-distance routes for walkers and cyclists criss-cross the country; among the most popular cycling routes are those along the Rhine, Mosel and Altmühl, while the Rennsteg ridgeline path in the Thuringian Forest is justly famous. In-line skating has risen dramatically in popularity in recent years, and provision is steadily increasing; a new 100-km (60-mile) route crosses the Fläming area south of Berlin.

For information about local hiking clubs and long-distance footpaths, contact the Verband Deutscher Gebirgs- und Wandervereine e.V. (National Association of Mountain and Hiking Clubs), <www.deutscher-wanderverband.de>. Tourist information centres can provide details of local route networks, and often have free maps.

Horse riding. Stables can be found in most holiday areas. For information, contact the **Deutscher Reiterliche Ver-**

Take a trip on a steamer down the Rhine – here at Cologne

einigung (National Riding Association), <www.hippoline. com>. You can get an overview of riding holidays at: <www.reiten.de>.

Water recreation. Lakes, rivers and canals form an extensive network of waterways, making cruising a practicable way of exploring much of the country *(see also page 168)*. The Mecklenburg lake district is particularly well suited to this sort of activity. Sailing enthusiasts will also enjoy the Mecklenburg lakes, as well as the broad waters of Lake Constance. The mountain areas nearly all provide opportunities for rafting, kayaking and canyoning. The breezy coasts of the North Sea and Baltic are wonderful for sailors and wind-surfers, with fjords and lagoons contrasting with more open waters. For information, contact the Deutscher Kanu-Verband (National Canoeing Association), <www.kanu.de>; the Deutscher Motoryachtverband (National Motorboating Association), <www.dmyv.de>; or the Deutscher Seglerverband e.V. (National Sailing Association), <www.dsv.org>.

Golf. Golfing has enjoyed a surge in popularity in recent years, with many courses laid out in beautiful surroundings. Guest players are usually welcome. Green fees in or near large cities can be expensive, but are much cheaper in the countryside. For information, contact the Deutscher Golf-Verband (National Golf Association), <www.golf.de>.

Angling. Trout is the favourite freshwater catch, and there's some good sea fishing along the coast. For information, contact the Deutscher Anglerverband (National Angling Association), <www.anglerverband.de>.

Climbing. The Bavarian Alps offer challenging climbing, with the possibility of staying at high altitudes in mountain huts. Rock climbers will find Germany's best rock faces in the sandstone formations of Saxon Switzerland. For information, contact the Deutscher Alpenverein (German Alpine Club), <www.alpenverein.de>.

Skiing in the Alps

Winter sports. Garmisch-Partenkirchen is Germany's winter sports capital, but opportunities to enjoy time in the snow abound throughout the Bavarian Alps, from Berchtesgaden in the east to the Allgäu in the west. Snowfall is more limited further north, but skiers head out of the cities to upland areas like the Taunus, the Black Forest and the Sauerland. Oberhof in the Thuringian Forest, once the GDR's prime winter resort, has particularly well-developed facilities, including a summer bobsleigh run. Information can be obtained from: <www.garmisch-partenkirchen.de>; <www.oberhof.de>; and from the Deutscher Skiverband (National Ski Association), <www.ski-online.de>.

Spectator Sports
Soccer. The huge resources put into the construction or renovation of stadiums across the country to host the 2006 World Cup are evidence enough of Germany's football fanaticism.

Although Germany's most popular sport is soccer, American football has a surprisingly large number of followers, and Germany has three teams competing in Europe's National Football League (NFL).

Millions of avid supporters watch the Saturday afternoon matches of the *Bundesliga*, Germany's national league, either in person or on TV. Passions reach fever pitch when the national team participates in the World Cup or the European Championship, each held every four years – 2006/2010 for the former and 2008/2012 the latter.

Ice hockey. Second only to soccer in popularity, ice hockey is played throughout the country, with professional teams competing in the national league, the *Deutsche Eishockey Liga*. The season runs from September to April.

Tennis. Stars like Boris Becker, Steffi Graf and Michael Stich have helped make tennis one of Germany's most popular spectator sports. The climax of the tennis season is the German Masters championship, held annually in Hamburg.

Basketball. Like soccer, basketball has its own *Bundesliga*, in which teams compete between October and April.

Motor racing. Germany hosts not one, but two Grand Prix events every year, one at the tortuous Nurbürgring in the Eifel uplands, the other at Hockenheim near Heidelberg.

Horse racing. The most prestigious meetings are the Düsseldorf Galopp – established in 1844 – and those held several times a year at Baden-Baden's Iffezheim racecourse.

SHOPPING

Germany has a well-earned reputation for high-quality manufactured goods, and a stroll around any large department store will reveal any number of consumer desirables. There are also plenty of tacky souvenirs. Most German town centres have been comprehensively pedestrianised, and as a result the traffic-free shopping experience can be quite pleasant, with attractive places to sit and recover while you ponder the wisdom of your purchases.

As elsewhere, chain stores and department stores occupy the prime sites, while humbler establishments like antiques shops and second-hand book dealers can be found in side streets, or in particular parts of town. The *Antik und Flohmarkt* beneath the railway arches near to Berlin's Friedrichstrasse is a treasure trove of antiques. Modern shopping arcades – *Passagen* – are often very inviting, especial-

Galeries Lafayette in Berlin

ly in the biggest cities; Berlin has state-of-the-art examples opening off redeveloped Friedrichstrasse, and there are other fine ones in Hamburg and Düsseldorf. Large, no-frills supermarkets and warehouse-type establishments cluster on the edges of towns, usually close to an *Autobahn* interchange, and they frequently offer very good value for everyday purchases.

Markets are great for people-watching as well as bargain-hunting; Munich's Viktualienmarkt is one of the city's great sights. Flea markets like the weekend one in Berlin's Charlottenburg are a great attraction, while Christmas markets, such as the ones in Nuremberg and Dresden, are full of atmosphere as well as good places for presents. Museum shops are well-stocked, often with original items unobtainable elsewhere.

Traditional wooden nutcracker

Things to Buy

Antiques. The prosperous periods in German history produced many fine goods, notably during the *Jugendstil* (the local version of Art Nouveau) and Art Deco eras. Ceramics and lamps are often of a very high quality and are available at reasonable prices. Early 19th century *Biedermeier* furniture is also very desirable.

Books. City bookshops are often palatial places, offering coffee and places to sit and read, as well as books, quite a few of them in English.

Fashion. Everything is available, from designer fashions to secondhand chic. Traditional Bavarian wear can look very smart in Bavaria, but how often would you sport *Lederhosen* or a *Dirndl* at home? A loden coat, made with the coarse, oily wool of mountain sheep, could be a better buy. Leatherwear is usually of a high quality.

Food and drink. Bakeries and delicatessens are of a high standard, though there are obvious problems in getting perishable items home. Visitors with a car will be tempted to load up with excellent and inexpensive beer, wine or spirits.

Porcelain. This long-established industry is still turning out fine products. Among the leading factories are Nymphenburg and Rosenthal, Meissen (both in Munich), KPM in Berlin, and Villeroy & Boch at Mettlach in the Saarland.

Souvenirs. As well as cuckoo clocks, timepieces of all kinds are made in the Black Forest. Germany is the natural habitat of the garden gnome and of the beer *Stein*.

Toys. Germans have traditionally been great toymakers, with centres of excellence in Nuremberg (mechanical toys, including the world's best model railways) and the Erzgebirge mountains in Saxony (carved items).

ENTERTAINMENT

In the form of classical music, opera, drama and dance, high culture prospers in Germany, not least because of generous government and municipal subsidies; German cities compete with one another in terms of cultural offerings, a situation which has resulted in the country having well over 100 opera houses. But popular culture and entertainment is vibrant as well; committed ravers will find their needs satisfied, particularly in the big cities and above all in Berlin, where clubs and other venues cater for every possible taste. Local papers and tourist information centres provide information, and some cities publish useful listings magazines.

The Munich Philharmonic

Music, opera, theatre. In the homeland of Bach, Beethoven and Brahms, every place of any size has a programme of opera and classical music concerts. Some of the venues, like Dresden's monumental Semperoper, are visitor attractions in their own right. In addition to purpose-built halls, concerts may be held in a historic church, like Bach's Thomas-kirche in Leipzig. Regular concerts take place through most of the year, with the summer break often being filled with a music festival. For non-German-speakers, the appeal of theatre is obviously limited, but ballet and modern dance is well developed, and English-language performances can sometimes be found. The appeal of musicals is universal, as are the lavish revues staged at venues like Berlin's Friedrichstadtpalast.

Rock, pop, jazz. The larger cities offer the biggest names and the broadest range, but rock, pop and jazz can be found virtually everywhere in Germany.

Brass bands. Oompah bands still dominate the scene in Bavarian beer halls, at the Munich Oktoberfest, and at the Karneval celebrations in the Rhineland and elsewhere.

Nightlife. Clubs and discos abound, some of the best in university cities, where there may be a popular student

The beer tents are crowded at the Oktoberfest

gathering place like the Moritzbastei in Leipzig. Sharp and witty cabaret is a German speciality.

Cinema. Movie-houses range from multiplexes to small art-house establishments. English-language films are usually dubbed into German, though one or two cinemas in larger centres will show films in the *Originalversion* ('OV'). Global marketing ensures that the latest Hollywood blockbusters are screened almost as soon as they are released in the US.

CHILDREN'S GERMANY

You only need to observe the generous provision in cities of playgrounds and other facilities for children to realise that children are as well catered for in Germany as anywhere. And traffic-free town centres and good footpath and cycle networks also help to make the urban environment relatively child-friendly. Children from countries where trams are a novelty may enjoy riding round town aboard a *Strassenbahn*. With an abundance of lakes and rivers, and mountains with chairlifts, cable-cars, and at the Brocken, a steam railway, there's usually plenty to do in the German countryside, to say nothing of the seaside with all its attractions and activities.

Museums. Museums will help keep children occupied and entertained, particularly those with plenty of interactive exhibits like Munich's Deutsches Museum *(see page 112)*, or those with huge model railways like Nuremberg's Transport Museum *(see page 123)*. The Chocolate Museum in Cologne *(see page 83)* is also a sure winner. Many museums have special programmes for children, though a knowledge of German is usually required.

Zoos. There are several world-class zoos in Germany, among them Hellabrunn in Munich and Berlin's Zoologischer Garten *(see page 34)*. The Zoo am Meer in Bremerhaven *(see page 49)* focuses on sea creatures and animals from the Arctic.

Theme parks. Germany's largest theme park is Europa-Park (open daily 9am–6pm; admission fee) near Freiburg, with a spectacular roller-coaster, closely followed by the likes of Phantasieland *(see page 83)* near Cologne and Belantis (open daily 10am–6pm; admission fee) outside Leipzig.

FESTIVALS

Drawing on local and regional traditions, Germany has an extraordinary range of popular festivals. Many are based on the church calendar, others on historical events, which may be lavishly re-created like the July *Kinderzeche* in Dinkels-bühl *(see page 127)*. Among the best known are the Oktober-fest in Munich *(see page 107)*, and Karneval in the Rhineland *(see page 83)*, but there are greater and lesser events throughout the country and during the course of the year. Their number has been augmented by recent innovations such as Berlin's Love Parade, so controversial that it had to be cancelled in two successive years. *Schützenfeste* – marksmen's festivals – are held in many places, mainly as an excuse for general revelry, with the largest taking place in Hanover in July. Music festivals tend to be staged in the summer months: among the most popular are those celebrating Beethoven in Bonn (September to October) and Wagner in Bayreuth (July). Some of the most spectacular events are those only put on at infrequent intervals, like the Landshut Wedding (every four years – next in 2009) and the Oberammergau Passion Play (every 10 years – next in 2010).

Love Parade participants

Calendar of Events

February: *Internationale Filmfestspiele Berlin*: Berlin International Film Festival. *Karneval:* Cologne stages the most spectacular pre-Lenten carnival, closely followed by those of Mainz and Düsseldorf; in the southwest the event is known as *Fastnet*, in which people wear grotesque masks, Rottweil being the most important centre.

February/March: Kurt Weill festival in Dessau.

Easter: Easter processions and Easter egg decoration in the Sorb areas of eastern Germany.

April: Devils and witches revel on *Walpurgisnacht* (30 April) in the Harz Mountains.

May: Start of Sunday costume plays (they run until September) in Hamelin celebrating the *Rattenfänger* (rat-catcher).

May/June: Re-creation of the *Meistertrunk* in Rothenburg-ob-der-Tauber on Whitsun weekend.

June: *Kieler Woche:* Kiel Week sailing regatta.

July: Ulm *Schwörmontag* river pageant. Heidelberg castle illuminations and fireworks display (also in June and September). Wagner festival in Bayreuth (always begins on 25 July and ends on 28 August). Love Parade in Berlin. *Kinderzeche* in Dinkelsbühl. Rhine in Flames illuminations and fireworks in Bingen/Rüdesheim.

August: Hamburg DOM Festival, one of the largest funfairs in Germany (also held in March/April and November). Rhine in Flames illuminations and fireworks in Koblenz. Fürth-im-Wald *Drachenstich* (Sticking the Dragon) pageant. *Gäubodenfest* beer festival in Straubing.

September/October: Rhine in Flames illuminations and fireworks in St Goar. Wine festivals throughout Germany. Beethoven festival in Bonn. *Berliner Festwochen*: A major international festival of opera, theatre, dance, music and art held in Berlin. Berlin Marathon begins and ends at the Brandenburg Gate. *Oktoberfest* beer festival in Munich, lasting 16 days up to the first Sunday in October; don't miss the colourful opening procession *(see page 107)*.

December: Christmas markets in Nuremberg and elsewhere.

EATING OUT

Traditional German cuisine is unfussy, prepared from a limited range of good ingredients, with an emphasis on nourishing soups, and quantities of meat, potatoes, dumplings and various kinds of cabbage. It is satisfying, if unsubtle. More recently, *Neue deutsche Küche* – new German cooking – has extended the range, lightened the preparation and reduced amounts. In addition, foreign cuisines have been enthusiastically adopted, making eating out in Germany an enjoyable, varied, and often inexpensive experience.

To accompany the meal, there is, of course, beer, Germany being one of the world's great brewing nations. The country's numerous breweries turn out distinctive products, often with a strongly regional character. But this is also a

Lunchtime in Munich

wine country, producing mainly white wines, but with a number of palatable reds, as well as *Sekt*, the local equivalent of champagne.

WHEN TO EAT

Breakfast *(Frühstück)* can be quite substantial, with cereal, protein in the form of soft- or hard-boiled eggs, cheeses and slices of cold meat or sausage, various kinds of bread ranging from chewy pumpernickel to crisp white rolls, yoghurt or *Quark* (cottage cheese), and fruit. There will normally be coffee to drink, though tea and fruit juices will also be available. Many Germans rise early and lunch late, so a *zweites Frühstück* – a second breakfast – is sometimes indulged in to fill the mid-morning gap, consisting of a filled roll or something similar.

  Lunch *(Mittagessen)* is traditionally the main meal of the day, attended by all members of the family, and consists of soup, a main course and dessert. Classic main dishes are often pork-based, with *Schnitzel* – a thin slice of meat coated in breadcrumbs – featuring prominently. The ubiquitous potato is treated in various ways, the tastiest being pan-fried *Bratkartoffeln*, sometimes accompanied by onions and fatty bacon cubes. The favourite vegetable is *Kraut* – cabbage – in the form of *Sauerkraut* or perhaps *Rotkohl* – red cabbage. Dessert could consist of *Quark* with some sort of fruit compote. Busy people are tending to cut back on lavish lunches in favour of lighter midday meals, leaving more ambitious eating to the evening.

  Dinner *(Abendessen* or *Abendbrot)* is for many people a relatively light and modest meal, with much use made of bread, accompanied by cheese, cold cuts, potato salad and various condiments such as pickled gherkins. Nowadays there is a tendency to make dinner the main meal of the day, with several courses and more lavish helpings.

WHAT TO EAT

German Specialities

Brot. Germany has successfully resisted the spread of taste-less white sliced bread, and the products of German bakeries are one of the country's glories. There are any number of different types of bread, but the commonest is *Landbrot*, usually made from rye and wholemeal flour, rather grey in colour, but aromatic and with a full, satisfying taste. Whole-grain *Vollkornbrot* is heavier and darker and even better-tasting, while *Pumpernickel* is denser and darker still. The best white bread comes in the form of rolls.

Fisch. Ocean fish are readily available, but perhaps the most characteristic fish dishes are those made from freshwater species, among them *Forelle* (trout) and *Zander,* a larger, and to most palates tastier fish, usually translated as pike-perch.

Kartoffeln. Enthusiastically promoted by none other than Frederick the Great, the humble potato appears frequently and in many forms as well as the ubiquitous *Bratkartoffeln* described above. *Salzkartoffeln* are ordinary boiled potatoes, while *pommes frites* – often simply referred to as *pommes* – have gained in popularity. When mashed, potatoes are called *Kartoffelbrei* or *Püree*. Grated, mixed with onion, pressed into thin cakes and crisply fried, *Kartoffelpuffer* are almost a meal in their own right. *Kartoffelsalat*, potato salad, is a popular accompaniment to a sausage meal.

Spätzle. An alternative to potato, at least in the southwest, is pasta or noodles, which go under the name of *Spätzle*, literally 'little sparrows'.

Knödel. Another alternative to the potato to help bulk out a meal is the dumpling, called *Klösse* in northern Germany, and *Knödel* in the south. Dumplings can be made with flour, white bread or potato. *Leberknödel* are liver dumplings, the essential ingredient of *Leberknödelsuppe*, a broth-like soup.

Spargel. The *Spargelzeit*, the asparagus season, begins in May. The Germans have devised a way to grow asparagus that eliminates sunlight from reaching the stalks: once sunlight is removed the plants do not produce chlorophyll, and so are white. The spears develop a milder flavour and there is an increase in the sugar content. Asparagus is eaten with various accompaniments or simply drenched in melted butter.

Wild. Many menus feature *Wild* – wild food or game. *Reh* (venison), *Kaninchen* or *Hase* (rabbit), *Wildschwein* (boar) and *Fasan* (pheasant) are all popular, often served in a rich sauce.

Wurst. It is impossible to exaggerate the importance of the *Wurst* – sausage – in German food culture. There are some 1,500 varieties of sausage, and a glance at the delicatessen counter of a large store such as Berlin's KaDeWe confirms that this is no exaggeration. Not merely a snack or a clever way of using parts of the animal which might otherwise be unappetising, a sausage can form the centrepiece of a meal. The more famous varieties include *Thüringer* from Thuringia, given extra piquancy by a shot of blood; *Nürnberger* from Nuremberg, a thin and particularly tasty sausage; and *Weisswurst* from Munich, a blander product based on veal. Then there are various kinds of slicing sausage, like *Mett-*

Nürnberger Bratwurst

wurst or *Cervelat*, while German salami compares favourably with the Hungarian version. Spreading sausages include *Teewurst* and *Leberwurst*, the latter coming in fine or coarse versions, with the best varieties bearing comparison with *foie gras*. The *Bockwurst*, known to the world as the Frankfurter, is boiled before serving, while the more interestingly textured *Bratwurst* is grilled or fried. *Blutwurst* – black pudding – is probably best consumed in small quantities, at least by the uninitiated. An essential accompaniment to most sausages is a generous helping of mild German mustard.

Regional Tastes

The regions of Germany, and even individual cities, are proud of their innumerable local specialities. Some have a strictly regional popularity, while others have become popular all over the country and can be obtained anywhere.

Eisbein. A boiled pork knuckle, a Berlin favourite. Seemingly impossible to tackle at one sitting, it can in fact be dealt with by removing the substantial quantities of fat. The accompanying sauerkraut helps cut through the residual grease. In Bavaria it's roasted and called *Schweinshax'n*.

Himmel und Erde. The Rhineland's 'Heaven and Earth' is a mixture of apples (which grow high up) and potatoes (from deep in the ground), usually served with frankfurters.

Kassler Rippchen. From Berlin, this is a pork chop, lightly salted, pickled in brine and then smoked.

Königsberger Klops. Meatballs made from minced beef and pork. The recipe comes from Königsberg (Kaliningrad), once capital of the province of East Prussia, an area now divided between Poland and Russia.

Labskaus. Originally a fisherman's breakfast, this monster mixed dish from the North Sea coast consists of mashed-up salt beef or corned beef, pickled herrings, beetroot, onions and pickles, topped by a fried egg.

Zwiebelkuchen, served with new wine and popular in the southwest

Leberkäse. Bavarian meat loaf made from minced cured pork, steamed and then baked to give it a crisp crust.

Leipziger Allerlei. 'Leipzig Hotchpotch' is an appetisingly colourful mixture of young vegetables, eaten as a snack on its own or as an accompaniment to a portion of meat.

Maultaschen. The German equivalent of ravioli, this Swabian speciality consists of little parcels of pasta stuffed with a mixture of minced pork and veal.

Sauerbraten. From the Rhineland, this consists of pot-roasted beef slices in a marinade featuring redcurrant jam, cream and onions among other ingredients.

Saumagen. Ex-Chancellor Helmut Kohl's favourite dish from his native Rheinland-Pfalz, 'sow's belly' is much nicer than it sounds, a delicious meat loaf of minced, spiced pork presented in slices.

Zwiebelkuchen. Traditional flan made with onions and served with new wine, from Hessen and Baden-Württemberg.

Desserts

Given the substantial character of most meals, sweet things tend to be relegated to the afternoon cup of coffee, and a meal might simply be finished off with a piece of fruit or fruit compote. However, there are several types of pudding which are more or less unique to Germany. In the south, *Mehlspeisen* – desserts made from flour – include steamed dumplings brushed with cinnamon or poppy seeds and *Krapfen*, a kind of doughnut. In the north, *Rote Grütze* consists of a compote of red fruits like redcurrants, strawberries, raspberries and cherries, mixed with sago or tapioca and served with cream, ice cream or vanilla sauce.

Some of the best bakery products only appear in the run-up to Christmas, among them the famous Nuremberg *Lebkuchen* – discs of glazed gingerbread – and the Dresden fruitcake known as *Stollen*.

WHAT TO DRINK

Beer

German beer is still brewed according to the ancient *Reinheitsgebot*, the Purity Law of 1516 which insisted on the use of a limited number of ingredients – hops, malt, yeast, barley and water – and nothing else. Beer drinkers tend to be faithful to the product of their local brewery, though some brands, like Bitburger from Bitburg in the Eifel uplands, have a national profile as a result of intensive marketing.

In some places, beer is brewed according to the season. Munich produces *Märzenbier* ('March beer'), while Berlin's tingling summer drink is *Berliner Weisse*, a pale beer with a shot of concentrated fruit juice.

Given the quality of German beers, few natives see

any reason for drinking imported beers, though exotica like Guinness have their adherents when there is no local equivalent.

Most German beers are of the Pilsner type: pale, bottom-fermented brews with a sharp, hoppy taste. Lighter beers with a milder taste are called *Helles*, and dark beers – *Dunkles* – can also be had. As elsewhere in the world, beer served on draught is often superior to the bottled product.

Munich is generally regarded as the capital of German beer, not least because of its thriving beer-hall culture. But some of the most

Weissbier and pretzels

characterful beers are those from the big breweries in the Ruhr industrial area, originally intended to slake the formidable thirst of coal miners and steel workers.

Nearby Düsseldorf takes great pride in its distinctive *Alt*, not unlike British bitter, and usually served in small glasses. With more breweries per population than anywhere else in the country and its own beer-hall traditions, Cologne offers a not dissimilar product, *Kölsch*, served in the same kind of thin glass. The little town of Einbeck between the Harz and the River Weser had no fewer than 700 breweries in the Middle Ages, and gave the world the name 'Bock' beer. Bamberg is known for the very individual taste of its *Rauchbier*, smoke beer.

Wine

The reputation of German wine has fluctuated over the years, and many drinkers have dismissed it out of hand as sweet, bland or characterless. This might apply to exported blended brands such as Liebfraumilch, but most German wine nowadays is at the very least drinkable, and in many cases superb.

It is worthwhile paying attention to the label before buying or ordering a bottle of wine. Ordinary wines are classified as *Tafelwein* – table wine – which can be very ordinary indeed, especially if imported wines have been blended with it. *Deutscher Tafelwein* – made exclusively from German grapes – is likely to be more palatable, with *Landwein* – country wine – being better

Quality grapes

still. Superior wines are categorised as *Qualitätswein* – quality wine, with further sub-categories indicating geographical origin or ever finer characteristics: a *Spätlese* wine, for example, is made from late-harvested grapes and is likely to have a fuller flavour, while *Eiswein* – ice wine – is the most exclusive and expensive of all, being made from grapes which have been touched by frost, yielding a wine of extraordinarily intense taste. The most widely planted variety of grape is Müller-Thurgau, but the Riesling grape is rather more highly rated. Gewürztraminer grapes are used to make a wine with an aromatic, spicy taste.

The most productive wine regions are Moselle-Saar-Ruwer, the Rhine valley, the sunny south-facing Rheingau west of Wiesbaden, Rhein-Hessen, Rheinland-Pfalz, and Baden. Interesting wines, in distinctive bulbous flask-like bottles, come from the banks of the River Main in Franconia, while eastern Germany, surprisingly, has two fascinating wine regions, a tiny one along the River Saale near Naumburg, and the larger Saxon area along the River Elbe up and downstream from Dresden.

Sparkling wine – *Sekt* – is of very variable quality. The best will be a vintage product made exclusively from grapes grown in one of the country's designated wine-growing regions.

Spirits

Schnaps is the colloquial term used to describe Germany's widely drunk, colourless, grain spirits. Among the best are juniper-flavoured *Steinhäger* in its distinctive stone bottle and *Kümmel*, flavoured with caraway seeds. A glass of schnaps goes very well with an evening meal of pumpernickel and ham. *Weinbrand* is a fruit brandy, some of the best being made from cherries *(Kirschwasser)* and from Mirabelle plums *(Mirabellenwasser)*. Grape brandies range from the ultra-fiery to the velvety.

Kaffeetrinken

Kaffeetrinken – coffee drinking – is the equivalent of English afternoon tea, and presents an opportunity to indulge in one of the highlights of German cuisine – *Kuchen* and *Torten* – cakes and tarts or flans. Confounding foreigners' expectations of heaviness, these are made with light pastry and succulent fillings and are almost invariably fresh and delicious. The coffee is good too, full-flavoured but not bitter, going well with the little pot of cream or evaporated milk provided.

WHERE TO EAT

Traditional, inn-like eating places which welcome drinkers as well as diners are variously described in German as *Gaststätte*, *Gasthof* or *Wirtschaft*. Another type of establishment where good German food is served is the *Ratskeller*, the vaulted and often very atmospheric cellars beneath the town hall, where the mayor would not be ashamed to entertain his guests. A *Restaurant* may or may not be more refined. Restaurants serving foreign food have increased greatly in number, and in the big cities most international cuisines are represented, perhaps with more emphasis on Turkish and Balkan food than elsewhere in Europe. Most establishments have a *Tageskarte* – menu of the day – offering good value for two or three courses.

If it is just a snack that is required, the place to look out for is the *Imbissstube*. These booths or stands deal in such staples as a sausage served on a paper plate and accompanied by a bread roll and as much mustard as required.

An eating place may be divided into a bar close to the entrance and a dining area beyond. A large table by the bar may well be the *Stammtisch*, kept jealously for local regulars. If an establishment is busy, it is quite acceptable to share a table with other guests, though not without first asking *Ist hier frei?* Etiquette demands that fellow-diners are wished *Guten Appetit!* as they start their meal, and *Auf Wiedersehen!* as they leave.

To Help You Order

Waiter/waitress, please!	**Bedienung, bitte.**
Could I/we have a table?	**Ich hätte/Wir hätten gerne einen Tisch.**
The bill, please.	**Zahlen, bitte.**
I would like…	**Ich möchte gerne…**

beer	**Bier**	menu	**Speisekarte**
bread	**Brot**	milk	**Milch**
coffee	**Kaffee**	mineral	**Mineral-**
dessert	**Nachtisch**	water	**wasser**
fish	**Fisch**	potatoes	**Kartoffeln**
fruit	**Obst**	salad	**Salat**
fruit juice	**Fruchtsaft**	soup	**Suppe**
glass	**Glas**	sugar	**Zucker**
ice cream	**Eis**	tea	**Tee**
meat	**Fleisch**	wine	**Wein**

... and Read the Menu

Aal	eel	**Lamm**	lamb
Apfel	apple	**Linsen**	lentils
Apfelsine	orange	**Nieren**	kidneys
Backhuhn/	roast	**Pfirsich**	peach
Brathuhn	chicken	**Pflaumen**	plums
Birne	pear	**Pilz**	mushroom
Blumenkohl	cauliflower	**Pute/**	turkey
Bohnen	beans	**Truthahn**	
Ei/Eier	egg/Eggs	**Rind**	beef
Eintopf	thick soup	**Rollmops**	pickled
Ente	duck		herring
Erbsen	peas	**Rosenkohl**	Brussels
Erdbeeren	strawberries		sprouts
Gans	goose	**Sahne**	cream
Gurke	gherkin	**Schinken**	ham
Himbeeren	raspberries	**Schwein**	pork
Hummer	lobster	**Speck**	bacon
Kalb	veal	**Spinat**	spinach
Kirsche	cherries	**Zunge**	tongue
Knoblauch	garlic	**Zwetschgen**	plums
Lachs	salmon	**Zwiebel**	onion

HANDY TRAVEL TIPS

An A–Z Summary of Practical Information

A

ACCOMMODATION *(Unterkunft)* (See also CAMPING, YOUTH HOSTELS and RECOMMENDED HOTELS)

Germany offers everything from world-class luxury hotels to humble hostels. Hotel chains are well represented, many of them with familiar names, others whose operations are restricted to Germany and perhaps the neighbouring countries. Rates compare favourably with those of other European countries, and the vast majority of establishments are spotless, well-maintained and run to high professional standards.

More information about accommodation can be obtained from the Hotel Verband Deutschland (<www.iha-hotelfuehrer.de>) and the German National Tourist Office (<www.germany-tourism.de>). The tourism departments of each *Land* publish lists of accommodation, as do local tourist information centres, whose staff will also locate a place to stay for a small fee.

Hotels *(Hotels)* are rated by the star system (1–4), which takes account of room sizes and facilities. Breakfast is normally included in the price. A *Hotel Garni* provides breakfast but not other meals. **Guest houses or inns** *(Gasthöfe, Gästehäuser, Pensionen)* are a simpler and cheaper alternative to hotels. **Bed and breakfast** *(Fremdenzimmer)* establishments are usually comfortable and clean, provide breakfast, and are a good way to meet local people. Staying at **self-catering** *(Ferienwohnungen, Ferienappartements)* establishments is a good way to minimise costs. **Camping and caravanning sites**, present throughout the country, are generally well run and laid out to a high standard (see also CAMPING, page 155). **Youth hostels** *(Jugendherberge)* are provided in profusion. See also YOUTH HOSTELS, page 171.

Do you have a single room/ double room?	**Haben Sie ein Einzelzimmer/ ein Doppelzimmer?**
What does the room cost?	**Was kostet das Zimmer?**

AIRPORTS *(Flughafen)*

Frankfurt has continental Europe's busiest airport, a national, international and intercontinental hub with excellent rail and road connections. Of Berlin's three airports, Tempelhof has been downgraded, Tegel continues to play the principal role, while Schönefeld (which served East Berlin) is being expanded. Other cities with international airports include Cologne-Bonn, Dresden, Düsseldorf, Hamburg, Hanover, Leipzig-Halle, Munich, Nuremberg and Stuttgart. A number of modestly equipped airports are used by international budget airlines, among them Erfurt (for Thuringia), Friedrichshafen (for Lake Constance), Hahn (for Frankfurt), Lübeck and Niederrhein (for the Lower Rhine area).

Where can I get a taxi?	**Wo finde ich ein Taxi?**
How much is it to the centre/	**Wieviel kostet es ins Zentrum?**
Does this bus go to the main railway station?	**Fährt dieser Bus zum Hauptbahnhof?**

B

BICYCLE HIRE *(Fahrradverleih)*

Enquire about bicycle hire at the local tourist information centre or look in the *Gelbe Seiten* (Yellow Pages) under FAHRRADVERLEIH. German Railways have a bike hire service in Berlin, Cologne, Frankfurt and Munich, tel: 01805 15 14 15. General information on cycling in Germany may be obtained from the Allgemeiner Deutscher Fahrrad-Club (National Cycle Club), <www.adfc.com>.

BUDGETING FOR YOUR TRIP

With its high standard of living, Germany is commonly thought of as an expensive country. However, while there may not be many outright bargains, the quality of goods and services is almost always high, and most visitors feel they get good value for their money.

Accommodation. Hotels (double room per night): 5-star €200–350, 4-star €120–200, 3-star €70–120, 2- and 1-star €80 or less. Similar accommodation in a *Gasthof* or *Fremdenzimmer* costs €50–70. Rates may double during a trade fair. Campsite charges range between €3 and €12 per person and €3 and €8 per tent, with extra fees for a caravan or car. Youth hostels charge an average of around €15 per person.

Car hire. A small car will cost around €50 per day, €300 per week. (See also CAR HIRE, page 156.)

Meals. A decent two-course meal ordered from the *Tageskarte* could cost as little as €10, while a gourmet meal with wine at a sophisticated restaurant will cost upwards of €30.

Entertainment. Approximate prices are: cinema from €6 (reductions on some evenings), discotheque €4–12, theatre or opera €10 upwards (average around €25), amusement park adult €22 child €15.

Sightseeing. Entry to museums and similar establishments average around €5. Most museums grant free admission on certain days or at certain times, and there are reductions for children and students.

Taxis. A minimum fee of around €3.50 is usually charged, plus a charge per kilometre of about €1.30. Rates may increase at night and at weekends and there may be a charge for luggage.

C

CAMPING

Germany has over 2,000 official campsites, graded according to the facilities offered. Sites tend to be full in the holiday season, and it is prudent to reserve a pitch in advance. Camping outside official sites is frowned upon, though it may be tolerated. The permission of the landowner is essential. The German National Camping Club has a useful website: <www.camping-club.de>.

CAR HIRE (See also DRIVING)

All the major international car-hire companies operate in Germany, with desks at airports, in city centres and at main railway stations. Local firms can be contacted through your hotel or by referring to the Yellow Pages under AUTOVERMIETUNG.

To hire a car you will normally need to be over 21 and to have held a valid driving licence for at least one year. An international licence is not necessary for visitors from EU countries, Canada or the USA. Insurance is compulsory and it is prudent to take out full cover. A deposit is not necessary if payment is being made by credit card.

I'd like to rent a car	**Ich möchte bitte ein Auto mieten.**
tomorrow	**für morgen**
for one day/week	**für einen Tag/für eine Woche**
Please include full insurance.	**Bitte schliessen Sie eine Vollkaskoversicherung ab**.

CLIMATE

Germany has a continental climate tempered by Atlantic influences. This gives warm, rather than extremely hot summers, and cool, rather than icy winters. Daily weather is variable, and there are pronounced regional differences. The northwest tends to have cooler summers and milder winters than the rest of the country. Rainfall occurs through-out the year, rising somewhat in the summer months, particularly in the south. The Alps are the wettest region and also experience the most snowfall, with ski slopes generally functioning between mid-December and March. Snowfall in other upland areas is less constant. Winds are strongest on the North Sea coast, while the warm, dry wind known as the *Föhn* blowing north from the Alps can create exceptionally clear conditions as well as causing headaches and even depression among those exposed to it. The best time to come to Germany is from May to September, though city visits can be made at any time. Popular tourist areas like the Rhine gorge can get very crowded at the height of summer. Sea-water temperatures rarely rise above 18°C (64°F).

CLOTHING *(Kleidung)*

The changeability of the weather means that you should pack clothes to match a variety of conditions. Even in summer, a waterproof outer garment is essential, with something warm for cool evenings. An umbrella will prove useful in most seasons. Bring a warm coat in winter.

Dress codes are fairly informal. Unless you are combining business with pleasure, a suit and tie can be left at home. Smart casual style will carry you through semi-formal occasions like the theatre or opera. Stout footwear is an asset for city sightseeing, and proper walking shoes or boots will enhance your enjoyment of mountain and forest walks.

CRIME AND SAFETY

The level of crime in Germany corresponds to the European average and presents no special problems to visitors, who simply need to take the usual precautions. These include leaving valuables in the hotel safe, being aware of pickpockets in crowded areas, and not leaving bags, cameras and similar objects unattended. Car theft is fairly common. Thieves should not be tempted by leaving items of interest on display in the car. Consider leaving the car in a guarded car park, especially overnight.

Report thefts and incidents to the nearest police station, and obtain written confirmation of lost items to make an insurance claim.

CUSTOMS AND ENTRY REQUIREMENTS

Visitors from EU countries only need an identity card (or passport) to enter Germany. Citizens of other countries, including the US, Canada, Australia and New Zealand, must have a valid passport. Nationals of other countries that do not have a reciprocal agreement with Germany need a visa. EU nationals may import duty-free goods for personal use. There is no limit on the amount of foreign currency that may be brought in and out of Germany.

I've nothing to declare.	**Ich habe nichts zu verzollen.**
It's for my personal use.	**Es ist für meinen persönlichen Gebrauch.**

D

DRIVING

To drive your own car in Germany you will need a valid driving licence, a vehicle insurance certificate, a red breakdown triangle, spare light bulbs and a first-aid kit. Non-EU citizens also need to bring the vehicle registration document.

Road conditions. The road network is well developed and maintained to a high standard, featuring a comprehensive network of toll-free *Autobahnen* (motorways) identified by numbers preceded by a letter A, and *Bundesstrassen* (federal main roads) identified by a letter B. Urban roads can be severely congested during rush hours, while the Autobahn can get crowded at holiday times. There is no general speed limit on the Autobahn, though there is an advisory limit of 130km/h (80mph). In built-up areas, indicated by a yellow place-name sign, the limit is 50km/h (31mph), elsewhere 100km/h (62mph). The use of front and rear seat belts is compulsory. Drive on the right and give way to traffic coming from the right unless on a road identified by a yellow diamond priority sign. Give way to passengers boarding or alighting at a tram stop. There are severe penalties for drinking and driving: the police may issue on-the-spot fines and may confiscate vehicles.

Petrol stations (usually self-service) are frequent and there is good provision of service and rest areas on the Autobahn.

Are we on the right road to ... ?	**Fahren wir richtig nach?**
Full tank please	**Volltanken bitte**
Please check the oil/tyres/battery	**Bitte kontrollieren Sie das Öl/die Reifen/die Batterie**

Parking *(Parken)*. Parking is strictly regulated, with no parking within 5m (5½yd) of a pedestrian crossing or road junction or within 15m (16½yd) of a bus or tram stop. On-street parking in towns is regulated by the standard blue P sign with times and conditions set out on a panel below. Payment is by ticket machine, parking meter and, in some places, by means of a parking disc obtained from shops or petrol stations.

Breakdowns and assistance. The warning triangle must be displayed to indicate a broken-down vehicle and hazard lights must be switched on. Assistance can be obtained by calling ADAC (German Automobile Club) on 01802 22 22 22. The police must be called on 110 if anyone is injured. The ambulance service and fire brigade can be reached on 112.

Road signs. You might come across some of the following:

Baustelle	Works/Construction site
Einbahnstrasse	One-way street
Einordnen	Get into lane
Fussgänger	Pedestrians
Glatteis	Icy surface
Langsam fahren	Drive slowly
Parkplatz	Car park
Rastplatz	Rest area
Stau	Congestion/Queue
Tankstelle	Petrol station
Umleitung	Detour
Vorsicht!	Take care!

E

ELECTRICITY *(Elektrizität, Strom)*

The standard is 220–250 volt, 50-cycle AC. Plugs are the continental type, and British and North American appliances need an adaptor.

EMBASSIES AND CONSULATES *(Botschaft; Konsulat)*

Contact your country's embassy or consulate if you lose your passport, have trouble with the authorities or suffer an accident. All embassies are in Berlin *(see list below)*. Britain, the US and Canada have consulates in Düsseldorf, Hamburg, Stuttgart and Munich; Britain and Australia have consulates in Frankfurt.

Australia: Wallstrasse 76–79, 10179 Berlin, tel: 030 88 00 88–0
Canada: Friedrichstrasse 95, 10117 Berlin, tel: 030 20 31 20
Ireland: Friedrichstrasse 200, 10117 Berlin, tel: 030 22 07 20
New Zealand: Friedrichstrasse 60, 10117 Berlin, tel: 030 20 62 10
South Africa: Tiergartenstrasse 18, 10785 Berlin, tel: 030 22 07 30
UK: Wilhelmstrasse 70–71, 10117 Berlin, tel: 030 20 45 70
US: Neustädtische Kirchstrasse 4–5, 10117 Berlin, tel: 830 50

Where is the British Embassy?	**Wo ist die britische Botschaft?**

EMERGENCIES

If you are at or close to your hotel and your command of German is less than fluent, it may make sense to seek help from the hotel reception. The following are the numbers for the emergency services:

Police 110; Ambulance 112; Fire 112

I need a doctor	**Ich brauche einen Arzt**
an ambulance	**einen Krankenwagen**
a hospital	**ein Krankenhaus**

ETIQUETTE (See also EATING OUT)

Behaviour in public is more formal than in Anglo-American countries. Hands are shaken when first meeting and possibly on parting. On entering a shop it is usual to say *'Guten Tag'*, and *'Auf Wiedersehen'* as you leave. A phone conversation is normally concluded with *'Auf Wiederhören'*, literally 'Until we hear each other again'. If invited home, be sure to bring a small gift, perhaps of flowers. Punctuality is highly rated.

G

GAY AND LESBIAN TRAVELLERS

Germany is one of the more tolerant countries for gays, though there are striking contrasts between acceptable behaviour in big cities and rural areas. Strongly conservative attitudes in the countryside, especially in Catholic Bavaria, mean that overt gayness is frowned on. At the other end of the spectrum, Berlin has a claim to be considered the gay capital of Europe, with traditions going back to the Weimar era as depicted in the novels of Christopher Isherwood. The 'scene' is vibrant, with numerous welcoming cafés, bars and clubs, and high-profile events like the Gay-Lesbian City-Festival in late June.

GETTING TO GERMANY

By air. There are direct flights from most European capitals and many other major cities to several airports in Germany (see also AIRPORTS). From North America, there are direct flights to Frankfurt from where there are connecting flights to all destinations. Budget airlines are steadily extending their operations, especially from the UK, and a number of smaller airports are served as well as the principal ones. The national airline is Lufthansa, <www.lufthansa.co.uk>.

By rail. The German rail network is linked to many European countries by direct trains. Eurostar trains from London connect at Brussels with German trains using the high-speed line to Cologne, where there are good connections to all major destinations in Germany. Luxurious sleeper trains run between Brussels and Berlin. DB (Deutsche Bahn; German Railways) has a very useful website, <www.bahn.de>.

By road. Germany is linked by good roads to all neighbouring countries. From Britain, the Channel Tunnel Shuttle and the Dover–Calais crossing are convenient for western and southwestern Germany. The overnight Harwich–Cuxhaven ferry brings northern and eastern Germany within easy reach (see <www.dfdsseaways. co.uk>). Other ferries from the UK serve Hook of Holland, Zeebrugge and Ostend.

GUIDES AND TOURS

Tourist information and marketing services are well developed, and English-speaking guides are available in most places. Details of tours may be provided in hotels, but local tourist information centres can offer a more comprehensive view of what is available. Walking tours of cities or parts of cities can be a fascinating alternative to the more conventional round trip (*Stadtrundfahrt*) by long-distance buses.

H

HEALTH AND MEDICAL CARE

Germany has reciprocal health-care arrangements with other EU countries including the UK. Medical treatment will normally be provided free of charge as long as you can produce a European Health Insurance Card (available from post offices in the UK and online at <www. ehic.org.uk>). Visitors from non-EU countries should check that their medical insurance covers them for travel in Germany, and even EU citizens may wish to insure themselves privately, for example to ensure prompt repatriation in a medical emergency.

In case of accident or serious illness, call the ambulance service on 112. Pharmacies (*Apotheken*) are open during normal shopping hours, and when shut display the address of the nearest one open.

HOLIDAYS *(Feirtage)*

Banks, post offices, government offices and many other businesses close on the following national holidays. There are also many regional and local holidays, several of them connected with events in the church calendar. Check with local tourist information centres.

1 January	**Neujahr**	New Year's Day
March/April	**Karfreitag,**	Good Friday,
	Ostermontag	Easter Monday
1 May	**Tag der Arbeit**	Labour Day
May	**Christi Himmelfahrt**	Ascension Day
May/June	**Pfingsten**	Whit Monday
3 October	**Tag der deutschen**	Day of German
	Einheit	Unity
25, 26 December	**Weihnachten**	Christmas

LANGUAGE

The national language of Germany is *Hochdeutsch* – High German – but distinctive regional and local dialects continue to be spoken in many areas, at least in informal settings. English is widely spoken or understood, particularly by people in the tourism and hospitality industries and by the young.

The *Berlitz German Phrase Book & Dictionary* covers most of the situations you are likely to encounter in Germany, and the German-English/English-German pocket dictionary contains a special menu-reader supplement and a short grammar section.

M

MAPS *(Karten)*

The local maps and town plans supplied free by tourist information centres, car-hire firms and some hotels and banks are often all you will need.

The 1:200,000 scale *Maxi-Atlas Deutschland,* published by ADAC (German Automobile Club) and available in the UK through the Automobile Association shows every road in the country. Other excellent maps and plans are available in bookshops and specialist map dealers.

MEDIA *(Medien)*

Radio and television. The BBC World Service can be found on a number of wavelengths including 90.2FM, and the British Forces Broadcasting Service broadcasts pop on BFBS 1 and magazine-style content including Radio 4 and Five Live on BFBS 2. German TV has two commercial-free national channels – ARD and ZDF – and several private and cable channels, while the satellite TV provided by most hotels invariably includes CNN and sometimes BBC World.

Newspapers and magazines. The leading serious daily newspapers are the FAZ – *Frankfurter Allgemeine Zeitung* – and the *Süddeutsche Zeitung* of Munich. The popular daily *Bild* leads the field in scandal and sensation. *Der Spiegel* is the most authoritative weekly. English-language publications like the *International Herald Tribune* are widely available, especially at newsstands in the larger cities.

MONEY *(Geld)*

The euro (EUR) is the official currency used in Germany. Notes are denominated in 5, 10, 20, 50, 100 and 500 euros; coins in 1 and 2 euros and 1, 2, 5, 10, 20 and 50 cents.

Banking hours are usually 9am–4pm Mon–Fri with a later opening to 6pm on one or two days a week, usually Thursday. Smaller establishments may close at lunchtime. Bureaux de change keep longer hours, and some are open 24/7.

Changing money. The easiest way to obtain euros is with a suitable debit/credit card at a cash machine (ATM). Most, but not all banks charge for this service. Foreign currency can be changed at an ordinary bank *(Bank)*, a savings bank *(Sparkasse)* or at a bureau de change *(Wechselstube)*. Hotels, post offices and travel agents also change money but rates are usually less favourable.

Credit cards are widely accepted but not to the same extent as in the US and UK, especially in smaller establishments.

VAT (value-added tax) can be refunded on purchases made by citizens of non-EU countries when they leave the country, provided documentation has been kept.

Can I pay with this credit card?	**Kann ich mit dieser Kreditkarte bezahlen?**
I want to change some pounds/dollars.	**Ich möchte Pfund/Dollar wechseln.**
Can you cash a traveller's cheque?	**Können Sie einen Reisescheck einlösen?**
Where's the nearest bank/ currency exchange office?	**Wo ist die nächste Bank/ Wechselstube?**
Is there a cash machine near here?	**Gibt es hier einen Geldautomaten?**
How much is that?	**Wieviel kostet das?**

O

OPENING HOURS

Most shops open at 9am and close at 5pm or 6pm Monday to Friday, and close at 4pm or even earlier on Saturday; supermarkets and department stores keep longer hours. Most museums open at 9am or 10am until 5pm or 6pm, frequently later on one evening a week. Almost all are closed on Monday. Tourist information centres have variable hours; in smaller places they may close on Saturday afternoons as well as Sundays, while in large cities and popular tourist areas they may stay open late on weekdays and remain open on Sunday. For opening times of banks, see MONEY *(page 164)*.

P

POLICE *(Polizei)*

The police wear green and khaki uniforms and drive white motorcycles and green and white patrol cars. They are armed, generally courteous and efficient if not particularly friendly, and are unbribable. The police emergency number is 110.

Where's the nearest police station?	**Wo ist die nächste Polizeiwache?**
I've lost my... wallet/bag/passport.	**Ich habe... mein Portmonnaie/ mein Tasche/ meinen Pass verloren.**

POST OFFICES *(Postamt)*

The Deutsche Bundespost (Federal Mail) is identified by its use of the colour yellow and its posthorn logo. Post offices are usually open Mon-–Fri 8am–6pm and Sat 8am–1pm. Smaller offices may close at lunchtime. For poste restante, letters should be marked *postlagernd*. If there is more than one slot in the yellow letter-boxes *(Briefkasten),* deposit non-local mail in the slot marked *Andere Postleitzahlen* or *Andere* PLZ.

Where's the nearest post office?	**Wo ist das nächste Postamt?**
express (special delivery)	**per Eilboten**
registered	**per Einschreiben**

PUBLIC TRANSPORT

Air. Major cities are connected by domestic flights, many of them operated by the national airline, Lufthansa. Timetables tend to favour business people, with early morning departures and evening returns.

Rail. DB (Deutsche Bahn) trains are generally very comfortable and reliable, and the rail network is comprehensive. A small number of lines are run by private operators. Types of train include: ICE (InterCity Express), a state-of-the-art train running at speeds of up to 319km/h (198mph); IC (InterCity), only marginally less up-to-the-minute; IR (Interregio), RE (RegionalExpress) and SE (StädteExpress) are modern trains filling in the gaps between ICE and IC services, while RB (RegionalBahn) stopping trains handle local services. Most services run at regular intervals (hourly or two-hourly) and the system is highly integrated.

Standard fares are not cheap, but there are many concessions and special tickets, among them the Euro Domino Pass giving unlimited travel for any three to eight days in any one month. A BahnCard giving substantial discounts on normal fares is really only useful for people travelling frequently in Germany. Weekend and regional tickets allow unrestricted travel within particular areas. Savings can also be made by purchasing a ticket in advance for a particular train at a particular time.

Navigating your way through these complexities is best done with the help of English-speaking staff at the *Reisezentrum* (travel centre) in all main stations. The DB website can be helpful too: <www.bahn.de>.

Bus. Long-distance bus services are relatively undeveloped in Germany. Bus lines fill in the gaps in the rail network and the Berlin Linien bus firm connects Berlin with most German cities.

Taxis. Taxi services are generally reliable and not over-expensive *(see* BUDGETING FOR YOUR TRIP, *page 154)*. Taxis, invariably painted cream, are to be found at taxi stands in prominent locations around town rather than by hailing them on the street.

Ferries and riverboats. Ferries are the usual way of getting to the islands off the North Sea and Baltic coasts. Ferries also operate at places along the Rhine and Elbe where there are no bridges. A trip on a white steamer along one of the main rivers is an essential component of a holiday in Germany, particularly on the middle Rhine (services operated by Köln-Düsseldorfer Rheinschiffahrt, <www.k-d.com>), the Mosel, the lower Neckar and the Elbe around Dresden (Sächsische Dampf-schiffahrt, <www.saechsische-dampfschiffahrt.de>).

City transport. Larger cities have integrated transport systems based on trams, S-Bahn (suburban railway), buses and, in the case of Berlin, Frankfurt, Hamburg and Munich, underground railways (U-Bahn). Trams *(Strassenbahn)* often run underground in city centres. Tickets are normally interchangeable between the different modes. Day, three-day and weekly passes are available, and in some cities there are 'Welcome Cards', which give free or reduced entry to a range of attractions as well as unrestricted travel. Underground stations are identified by a U on a white background, S-Bahn stations by an S on a white background, bus and tram stops by a green H on a yellow background. Tickets and passes are usually available from machines at stops and stations. After purchasing your ticket or pass, validate it by cancelling it in one of the machines provided, either at the stop or on board the vehicle.

What's the fare to ... ?	**Wieviel kostet es nach ...?**
Where is the nearest bus/ tram stop?	**Wo ist die nächste Bus/ Strassenbahn-Haltestelle?**
When's the next train to ...?	**Wann fährt der nächste Zug nach ...?**
I want a ticket to ... single/return	**Ich will eine Fahrkarte nach ... einfache Karte/Rückfahrkarte**
Will you tell me when to get off?	**Können Sie mir bitte sagen, wann ich aussteigen muss?**

R

RELIGION

The southern parts of the country tend to be mostly Roman Catholic, strongly so in Bavaria, while the north is mostly Protestant with the exception of the Rhineland. There are some three million Muslims in Germany, mostly of Turkish descent. The relatively few Jews are concentrated in the larger cities. Services in English can be found in Berlin and the larger cities.

T

TELEPHONE

Most telephone services are operated by the national company, Deutsche Telekom. The country code for Germany is 49. To call Germany from Britain, dial 00 49, then the area code omitting the zero, followed by the number. To call Britain from Germany, dial 00 44, followed by the local code minus the zero, then the number. For domestic enquiries, tel: 11 8 33; for international, tel: 11 8 34

Calls can be made from hotel rooms, but more cheaply from phone booths. Most of these accept phone cards in various denominations, and some accept credit cards. Phone cards can be obtained from post offices, newspaper kiosks and petrol stations.

Most British mobile phones will work in Germany, but check charges before leaving.

TIME ZONES

Germany follows Central European Time (GMT + 1 hour), and in summer an hour is added for Daylight Saving.

Auckland	Sydney	Jo'burg	**Berlin**	London	New York
10pm	8pm	noon	**noon**	11am	6am

TIPPING

In hotels, it is customary to leave a modest tip for the chambermaid and to tip the porters for bags carried. In restaurants, a service charge is normally included in the bill, but it is still usual to round up the amount you pay, though no more than 5 percent. For cloakrooms, where a charge is not made, small change is an apporopriate tip. Taxi drivers expect a 10 percent tip.

TOILETS *(Toiletten, WC)*

Provision of public toilets is generally good in Germany and facilities are well kept. Always have small coins ready in case the door has a coin slot. Male and female facilities are indicated by a symbol or by the words *Herren* (Gentlemen) and *Damen* (Ladies).

Where are the toilets?	**Wo sind die Toiletten?**

TOURIST INFORMATION OFFICES

The German National Tourist Board (GNTB) – Deutsche Zentrale für Tourismus e.V. (DZT) – can give you information on when to go, where to stay and what to see in Germany. The headquarters is located at: Beethovenstrasse 69, D-60325 Frankfurt-am-Main, tel: (069) 75 10 03, <www.germany-tourism.de>. The GNTB also maintains offices in many countries throughout the world:

Australia: GPO Box 1461, Sydney, NSW 2001, tel: 612 8296 0488

Canada: 480 University Avenue, Suite 1419, Toronto, Ontario, M5G 1V2, tel: 416 968 1685

UK: PO Box 2695, London W1A 3TN, tel: 020 7317 0908

US: 122 East 42nd Street, 20th Floor, Suite 2000, New York, NY 10168-0072, tel: 212 661-7200

PO Box 59594, Chicago, IL 60659-9594, tel: 773 539-6303

501 Santa Monica Boulevard, Suite 601, Santa Monica, CA 90401, tel: 310 394-2580

The German *Länder* and certain tourist regions have tourism marketing departments which can be useful sources of information for their areas. The GNTB can supply details of how to contact them. However, once in the country, your first port of call should be the local tourist information centre, to be found in every city and in most smaller towns. They are invariably well-stocked with information of all kinds, and almost always have helpful, English-speaking staff who can advise on what to do and provide details of guided tours. Many will book accommodation and sell tickets for events.

W

WEBSITES AND INTERNET CAFÉS

Internet cafés abound in major German cities, and can even be found in smaller places. An increasing number of hotels provide internet facilities.

All German towns have a website, often with an English version, on the pattern of <www.stuttgart.de>, with quick access to the kind of information useful in planning a visit.

Other websites include:

<www.germany-tourism.de> German National Tourist Board.

<www.germany-info.org> German Embassy website.

<www.bed-and-breakfast.de> Lists and categorises B&B establishments throughout Germany.

<www.hotelguide.de> Lists thousands of German hotels.

<www.bahn.de> German Railways (Deutsche Bahn) website.

<www.dertravel.net> Travel information and booking service of the long-established German national travel agency, DER.

YOUTH HOSTELS *(Jugendherberge)*

Germany's hundreds of youth hostels are listed in the directory published by the national hostelling association: Deutsches Jugendherbergswerk , Bismarckstrasse 8, 32756 Detmold, tel: 05231 740 10, <www.djh.de>. Book in advance in summer and at weekends.

Recommended Hotels

The following hotels in towns, cities and regions throughout Germany are listed under the major headings used in the Where to Go section. They include a number of modest but attractive establishments, as well as conventional luxury hotels. Advance booking is recommended, especially in summer. In cities such as Hanover, Cologne and Hamburg which have a programme of trade fairs, prices can double when a fair is in progress and accommodation will be difficult to find. Special deals are often available at weekends.

As a basic guide to prices for a double room with breakfast we have used the following symbols:

€€€€	over €210
€€€	€130–210
€€	€80–130
€	below €80

BERLIN AND POTSDAM

BERLIN

Adlon-Kempinski €€€€ *Unter den Linden 77, 10117 Berlin, tel: 030 22 61 11 11, <www.hotel-adlon.de>.* The new Adlon strives, with great success, to emulate the traditions of its legendary predecessor, the haunt of spies, diplomats and international celebrities that was burnt out in World War II and eventually demolished. The location, right by the Brandenburg Gate, could hardly be bettered, nor could the hotel's standards of service, facilities and comfort. 336 rooms.

Art Nouveau €€–€€€ *Leibnitzstrasse 59, 10629 Berlin, tel: 030 327 74 49, <www.hotelartnouveau.de>.* Excellent location just off Kurfürstendamm for this well-run establishment on the fourth floor of a stately century-old town house. Attractive bedrooms, some with antique furnishings. 22 rooms.

Art-Otel Berlin €€€ *Joachimsthaler Strasse 29, 10719 Berlin, tel: 030 88 44 70, <www.sorat-hotels.com>*. Centrally located on the fringe of the Zoo area, this was the first of Berlin's 'art hotels', with public spaces and bedrooms graced by artworks, fittings, and interior design by avant-garde figures such as Philippe Starck. 133 rooms.

Augustinenhof €€–€€€ *Auguststrasse 82, 10117 Berlin, tel: 030 30 88 60, <www.hotelaugustinenhof.de>*. Once a Christian hospice, this comfortable establishment in a side street just a short walk from Hackescher Markt is expertly run by the Berlin city mission. The attractive interiors feature contemporary abstract paintings. City tours on foot can be organised and there are reductions for train travel. 63 rooms.

Madison €€€€ *Potsdamerstrasse 3, 10785 Berlin, tel: 030 5900 50000, <www.madison-berlin.de>*. Lavishly equipped designer hotel with impeccable service in the Potsdamer Platz district. 166 rooms.

Q! €€€ *Knesebeckstrasse 67, 10623 Berlin, tel: 030 8100 660*. One of the latest additions to Berlin's growing range of distinctive, up-to-the-minute places to stay, this trendy, medium-sized Charlottenburg establishment boasts lavish facilities including an oriental-style wellness area. 77 rooms.

POTSDAM

Am Luisenplatz €€–€€€ *Luisenplatz 5, 14471 Potsdam, tel: 0331 97 19 00, <www.hotel-luisenplatz.de>*. In a convenient location between the centre of Potsdam and the park of Schloss Sanssouci, this elegant town hotel offers classically comfortable accommodation at reasonable rates. 30 rooms.

Schlosshotel Cecilienhof €€€–€€€€ *Neuer Garten, 14469 Potsdam, tel: 0331 3 70 50, <www.relaxahotels.de>*. The English-style country house built for Crown Prince Wilhelm in the lush parkland setting of Potsdam's Neuer Garten is now a luxury hotel frequented by presidents and prime ministers. The city centre is a short bus ride away, or it can be reached by walking along the lakeside. 42 rooms.

SPREEWALD

Schloss Lübbenau €€–€€€ *Schlossbezirk 6, 03222 Lübbenau, tel: 03542 87 30, <www.schlossluebbenau.de>*. With its comfortable rooms furnished in traditional style, this restored country seat makes an excellent base for exploring the delights of the watery countryside all around. It also has a choice of tempting places to dine. 46 rooms.

BALTIC COAST

Elisabeth von Eiken €–€€ *Dorfstrasse 39, 18347 Ostseebad Ahrenshoop, tel: 038220 69 90, <www.elisabethvoneiken.de>*. On the sandy Fischland peninsula, Ahrenshoop still retains the atmosphere of an early 20th-century artists' colony, nowhere more than in this lovely Art Nouveau villa adorned with artworks. 6 rooms.

Vier Jahreszeiten Binz €€€ *Zeppelinstrasse 8, 18609 Binz, tel: 038393 500, <www.vier-jahreszeiten.de/binz>*. Built in traditional style, this luxury hotel in the heart of Rügen Island's premier resort offers every comfort and a wide range of facilities and is within walking distance of promenade and pier. Gourmet restaurant. 76 rooms.

Strandhotel Ostseeblick €€€ *Kulmstrasse 28, 17424 Heringsdorf, tel: 038378 540, <www.strandhotel-ostseeblick.de>*. In the resort of Usedom Island, the award-winning 'Seaview' Hotel in as good as its name, with many of its rooms enjoying Baltic vistas. Lavish 'wellness' and beauty therapy facilities and gourmet restaurant. 61 rooms.

BREMEN

Hilton Bremen €€€€ *Böttcherstrasse 2, 28195 Bremen, tel: 0421 369 60, <www.bremen.hilton.com>*. Large hotel with all the usual Hilton amenities plus a city-centre location on the architecturally distinguished Böttcherstrasse. 235 rooms.

LÜBECK

Klassik Altstadt Hotel €€ *Fischergrube 52, 23552 Lübeck, tel: 0451 70 29 80, <www.klassik-altstadt-hotel.de>*. Small, family-run hotel in a fine old town mansion in a quiet location in the heart of the Hanseatic town. Attractive, comfortable rooms, themed to reflect prominent Lübeck personalities. Restaurant. 28 rooms.

HAMBURG

Vier Jahreszeiten €€€–€€€€ *Neuer Jungfernstieg 9–14, 20354 Hamburg, tel: 040 34940, <www.raffles.com>*. Overlooking the Binnenalster lake, the 'Four Seasons' is a grand hotel with all the amenities you would expect, including bedrooms furnished with antique pieces. The dining is among the best in town. 156 rooms.

Gastwerk €€–€€€ *Beim Alten Gaswerk 3, 22761 Hamburg, tel: 040 89 06 20, <www.gastwerk-hotel.de>*. Hamburg's first designer hotel is a successful combination of old architecture and contemporary style. It's in the suburb of Bahrenfeld only 4km (2½ miles) from the city centre, which is only minutes away by S-Bahn. 134 rooms.

Prem €€–€€€ *An der Alster 8–10, 20099 Hamburg, tel: 040 24 83 40 40, <www.hotel-prem.de>*. This small and immaculately run private establishment on the banks of the Alster prides itself on its service and on its attractive, individually furnished rooms. International and regional cuisine in a restaurant and a bistro. 48 rooms.

MECKLENBERG LAKE DISTRICT:

Ecktannen €€ *Fontanestrasse 51, 17192 Waren, tel: 03991 6290, <www.ecktannen.de>*. Idyllically located in the small town of Waren and convenient for all the recreational activities available on the water and in the surrounding area, this pleasant small hotel offers a friendly reception and attractive, inexpensive accommodation. 32 rooms.

ROSTOCK/WARNEMÜNDE

Hotel Sonne €€–€€€ *Neuer Markt 2, 18055 Rostock, tel: 0381 497 30, <www.rostock.steigenberger.de>.* This stylish establishment benefits from a central location on Rostock's market square and offers an excellent range of facilities. 124 rooms.

Wilhelmshöhe €–€€ *Waldweg 1, 18119 Diedrichshagen, tel: 0381 54 82 80, <www.ostseehotel-wilhelmshoehe.de>.* Friendly hotel amid lovely natural surroundings on the coast to the west of Warnemünde. Ask for a room with balcony facing the Baltic. 21 rooms.

DRESDEN AND THE TWO SAXONYS

DRESDEN

Kempinski Hotel Taschenberg Palais €€€€ *Taschenberg 3, 01067 Dresden, tel: 0351 491 20, <www.kempinski-dresden.de>.* Sumptuous palace in the very heart of Dresden, offering its guests every possible comfort and convenience. 214 rooms.

Romantik Hotel Pattis €€€ *Merbitzer Strasse 53, 01157 Dresden-Briesnitz, tel: 0351 425 50, <www.pattis.de>.* This establishment in Dresden's western suburb of Briesnitz has a gourmet restaurant complementing its attractive rooms and other lavish facilities. 46 rooms.

Schloss Eckberg €€€ *Bautzner Strasse 134, 01099 Dresden-Loschwitz, tel: 0351 809 90, <www.schloss-eckberg.de>.* Set in parkland, this romantic Gothic Revival castle stands on high ground overlooking the River Elbe. Varied styles of accommodation in tastefully furnished, comfortable rooms. 84 rooms.

LEIPZIG

Hotel Fürstenhof €€€–€€€€ *Tröndlinring 8, 04105 Leipzig, tel: 0341 1400, <www.arabellasheraton.com>.* Leipzig's centrally located, leading hotel is a renovated 18th-century palace offering the highest standards of service, facilities and comfort. 92 rooms.

Victor's Residenz-Hotel €€–€€€ *Georgring 13, 04103 Leipzig, tel: 0341 68660, <www.victors-leipzig.bestwestern.de>*. Opposite Leipzig's famous railway terminus and with all the attractions of the city centre within easy walking distance, this comfortable Best Western establishment makes an excellent base. 101 rooms.

SAXON SWITZERLAND

Romantik Hotel Tuchmacher €€ *Peterstrasse 8, 02826 Görlitz, tel: 03581 47310, <www.tuchmacher.de>*. Three restored Renaissance buildings amalgamated to form this comfortable and characterful hotel high above the River Neisse. The restaurant serves exquisite Silesian specialities. 30 rooms.

WEIMAR AND THURINGIA

EISENACH

Hotel auf der Wartburg €€€€ *Auf der Wartburg, 99817 Eisenach, tel: 03691 7970, <www.wartburghotel.de>*. Beneath the Wartburg Castle, this establishment offers supreme comfort as well as vistas over the Thuringian Forest. First-class restaurant. 35 rooms.

GOTHA

Landhaus Hotel Romantik € *Salzgitterstrasse 76, 99867 Gotha, tel: 03621 364 90, <www.landhaus-hotel-romantik.de>*. An attractive and inexpensive option, this family-run establishment is located on the eastern outskirts of the old ducal capital and has a courtyard terrace and a charming garden among its amenities. 14 rooms.

WEIMAR

Hotel Elephant €€€–€€€€ *Markt 19, 99423 Weimar, tel: 03643 8020 , <www.arabellasheraton.com>*. Weimar's most famous place to stay, in operation since 1696, though the opulent interiors now owe more to the age of Art Deco. Dine in the renowned Anna Amalia gourmet restaurant or, more affordably, in the rustic cellar. 102 rooms.

HANOVER AND THE HARZ

GOSLAR

Treff-Hotel Das Brusttuch €€ *Hoher Weg 1, 38640 Goslar, tel: 05321 346 00, <www.treff-hotels.de>*. This 500-year old mansion is richly ornamented and is located on the town's market square. An intimate hotel with a third-floor swimming pool. 13 rooms.

HANOVER

Kastens Hotel Luisenhof €€€–€€€€ *Luisenstrasse 1–3, 30159 Hannover, tel: 0511 304 40, <www.kastens-luisenhof.de>*. Centrally located between Hanover's opera house and the main railway station, this historic hotel is a city institution, offering its guests the best in comfort and range of facilities. Gourmet restaurant. 152 rooms.

QUEDLINBURG

Romantik Hotel Theophano €€ *Markt 14, 06484 Quedlinburg, tel: 03946 963 00, <www.hoteltheophano.de>*. Charming establishment consisting of three linked historic buildings on Quedlinburg's main square. Atmospheric cellar restaurant. 22 rooms.

WERNIGERODE

Gothisches Haus €€€ *Am Markt 1, 38855 Wernigerode, tel: 03943 63 90 05, <www.travelcharme.com/gotisches-haus>*. Historic 15th-century edifice on Wernigerode's marketplace offers every comfort as well as traditional atmosphere. Facilities include extensive 'wellness' area. Choice of restaurants. 116 rooms.

COLOGNE, THE RUHR AND RHINE

COLOGNE

Das Kleine Stapelhäuschen €€ *Fischmarkt 1–3, 50667 Köln, tel: 0221 25 77 862, <www.koeln-altstadt.de/stapelhaeuschen>*.

This narrow-fronted old edifice stands in Cologne's Altstadt right by the River Rhine. Characterful, highly individual rooms and a restaurant serving hearty food. 60 rooms.

Excelsior Hotel Ernst €€€€ *Trankgasse 1–5, Domplatz, 50667 Köln, tel: 0221 27 01, <www.excelsiorhotelernst.de>.* An oasis of tranquillity, this 150-year-old establishment is located right opposite the cathedral. Luxurious rooms are a tasteful blend of modernity and tradition. Gourmet restaurant. 152 rooms.

DÜSSELDORF

Orangerie €€–€€€ *Bäckergasse 1, 40213 Düsseldorf, tel: 0211 86 68 00, <www.hotel-orangerie-mcs.de>.* In a quiet part of the Altstadt free of through-traffic, this private hotel in an attractive neo-classical building offers stylish contemporary rooms. 27 rooms.

MÜNSTER

Hof zur Linde €€–€€€€ *Handorfer Werseufer 1, 48157 Münster-Handorf, tel: 0251 327 50, <www.hof-zur-linde.de>.* Just beyond the city limits and easily accessible from the Autobahn, this establishment's origins go back to the 17th century. Pleasant riverbank location and a choice of comfortable, characterful rooms and suites. 47 rooms.

THE RHINE

Bellevue-Rheinhotel €€–€€€ *Rheinallee 41–42, 56154 Boppard, tel: 06742 10 20, <www.bellevue-boppard.de>.* Sited on the riverside promenade of one of the Rhine gorge's most attractive towns, a stately establishment that is impeccably run. 94 rooms.

SOUTHWEST TO THE BLACK FOREST

BADEN-BADEN

Hotel am Markt €–€€ *Am Marktplatz 18, 76530 Baden-Baden, tel: 07221 270 40, <www.hotel-am-markt-baden.de>.* Family-run hotel in quiet location in Baden-Baden's Altstadt, with straight-forward but elegant rooms. 26 rooms.

FRANKFURT

Liebig-Hotel €€–€€€ *Liebigstrasse 45, 60323 Frankfurt-am-Main, tel: 069 72 75 51, <www.hotelliebig.de>.* Small hotel in an exclusive residential district in Frankfurt's west end, offering a choice between simply furnished and more elaborately decorated rooms at reasonable rates. 20 rooms.

Steigenberger Frankfurter Hof €€€€ *Am Kaiserplatz 1, 60311 Frankfurt-am-Main, tel: 069 215 02, <www.steigenberger.de>.* The listed Frankfurter Hof is a showcase for the prestigious Steigenberger hotel group, which has its headquarters here. Expensive, but everything a grand hotel should be. 332 rooms.

FREIBURG

Markgräfler Hof €€–€€€ *Gerberau 22, 79098 Freiburg im Breisgau, tel: 0761 325 40, <www.markgraeflerhof.de>.* Exquisite private hotel in a renovated neoclassical palace in Freiburg's 'Little Venice'. Comfortable, country-style rooms, wine bar and one of Freiburg's best restaurants. 15 rooms.

HEIDELBERG

Zum Ritter St Georg €€€ *Hauptstrasse 178, 69117 Heidelberg, tel: 06221 1350, <www.ritter-heidelberg.de>.* Stay in style on Heidelberg's main street, in one of the city's loveliest town mansions, dating from the late 16th century. The quieter rooms are in the modern extension to the rear. 39 rooms.

LAKE CONSTANCE

Hotel Löwen €€ *Marktplatz 2, 88709 Meersburg am Bodensee, tel: 07532 430 40, <www.hotel-loewen-meersburg.de>.* Five-hundred-year-old inn on the market square in the upper part of this lakeside town, with lots of atmosphere, attractive, comfortable rooms, and a panelled restaurant. 21 rooms.

STUTTGART

Ochsen €–€€ *Ulmer Strasse 323, 70327 Stuttgart-Wangen, tel: 0711 407 05 00, <www.ochsen-online.de>*. Family-run, timber-framed 18th-century inn close to the River Neckar and 15 minutes by public transport to the city centre. Stylish bedrooms, some with jacuzzi. 22 rooms.

MUNICH AND THE SOUTH

BAVARIAN ALPS

Vier Jahreszeiten €€–€€€ *Maximilianstrasse 20, 83471 Berchtesgaden, tel: 08652 95 20, <www.berchtesgaden.com/vier-jahreszeiten>*. Central hotel with attractive and comfortable pan-elled rooms, some with superb Alpine views. Breakfast terrace and indoor pool. 52 rooms.

Gasthof Frauendorfer € *Ludwigstrasse 24, 82467 Garmisch-Partenkirchen, tel: 08821 92 70, <www.gasthof-frauendorfer.de>*. Pleasantly rustic rooms in a charming old inn with typical Bavarian paintings. Folklore evenings in the equally rustic restaurant. 30 rooms.

MUNICH

Bayerischer Hof €€€€ *Promenadeplatz 2–6, 80333 München, tel: 089 21 200, <www.bayerischerhof.de>*. Family-run for over a century, this grand hotel is a city institution. Contemporary luxury in a traditional atmosphere. 395 rooms.

Gästehaus Englischer Garten €€ *Liebergesellstrasse 8, 80802 München, tel: 089 383 94 10, <www.hotelenglishgarden.de>*. Charming small establishment in a converted watermill right by Munich's largest park, the Englischer Garten. Book well in advance. 12 rooms, 17 apartments.

Kempinski Vier Jahreszeiten €€€€ *Maximilianstrasse 17, 80539 München, tel: 089 21 250, <www.kempinski-vierjahreszeiten.de>.* Munich's 'other' grand hotel, the haunt of celebrities since 1858, offering every amenity in the heart of the city. 316 rooms.

NUREMBERG AND NORTHERN BAVARIA

BAMBERG

Sankt Nepomuk €€–€€€€ *Obere Mühlbrücke 9, 96049 Bamberg, tel: 0951 984 20, <www.hotel-nepomuk.de>.* Converted mill and charming old annexes offer individually designed and furnished rooms of great comfort. 47 rooms.

GERMAN WINE ROUTE

Deidesheimer Hof €€–€€€ *Am Marktplatz 1, 67146 Deidesheim, tel: 06326 968 70, <www.deidesheimerhof.de>.* Tastefully furnished rooms in an establishment that is also one of Germany's gastronomic highspots. 28 rooms.

NUREMBERG

Agneshof €€€ *Agnesgasse 10, 90403 Nürnberg, tel: 0911 21 44 00, <www.agneshof-nuernberg.de>.* Centrally located in a side street, this medium-sized establishment offers attractive contemporary rooms – some with a view of the castle – and a courtyard garden. 72 rooms.

Bischofshof €€€ *Kräutermarkt 3, 93047 Regensburg, tel: 0941 584 60, <www.hotel-bischofshof.de>.* Former bishop's palace in the heart of Regensburg. Quiet, individually furnished rooms. 55 rooms.

ROTHENBURG-OP-DER-TAUBER

Hotel Markusturm €€–€€€ *Rödergasse 1, 91541 Rothenburg-ob-der-Tauber, tel: 09861 942 80, <www.markusturm.de>.* Intimate establishment in a building dating from the 13th century. Charming, individually furnished rooms. 25 rooms.

Recommended Restaurants

Below is a selection of restaurants mainly offering regional and local German specialities. Bear in mind that most establishments have a *Tageskarte* or *Menü* at lunchtime, which usually consists of a soup or hors d'oeuvres and a main course and offers a considerable saving over à la carte prices. It is not normally necessary to book a table in advance, but it is worthwhile checking locally beforehand whether this is advisable. Many restaurants have a weekly *Ruhetag* – day of rest – and may close for an annual holiday. Again, this should be checked.

The symbols below give some idea of the average cost of a meal for one, excluding drinks:

€€€ over €45

€€ €25–45

€ below €25

BERLIN AND POTSDAM

BERLIN

Hugos €€€ *Hotel Intercontinental, Budapester Strasse 2, 10787 Berlin, tel: 030 2602 1263.* Much-starred restaurant atop the high-rise Intercontinental Hotel with a view over the Tiergarten and much of the city. Mediterranean-inspired food of the very highest quality.

Leibniz-Klause €–€€ *Leibnizstrasse 46, 10623 Berlin, tel: 030 323 70 68.* Award-winning establishment successfully combining the functions of an above-average pub and excellent restaurant. Sophisticated German and international cuisine. Open noon–1am.

Marjellchen €–€€ *Mommsenstrasse 9, 10629 Berlin, tel: 030 883 26 76.* Filling food based on the traditional cuisine of Germany's former eastern provinces. Warm welcome and cosy atmosphere in the heart of Charlottenburg. Open Mon–Sat 5pm–midnight.

Opernpalais Unter den Linden €–€€€ *Unter den Linden 5 (next to Staatsoper),10117 Berlin, tel: 030 20 26 83.* A wonderful range of food and drink, from refined German cuisine in the Fridericus restaurant to coffee and delicious cakes in the Operncafé. The terrace is a place to see and be seen. Open 9am–midnight.

Ständige Vertretung € *Schiffbauerdamm 8, 10117 Berlin, tel: 030 282 39 65.* Lively, high-ceilinged establishment on the quayside serves Rhineland specialities best washed down with a glass or three of hoppy *Kölsch* beer from Cologne. The decor makes much play with the restaurant's political connections. Open 10am–midnight.

POTSDAM

Krongut Bornstedt € *Ribbeckstrasse 6/7, 14469 Potsdam, tel: 0180 576 6488.* Lovingly restored group of early 19th-century buildings which have been adapted to house craft workshops and boutiques as well as a couple of cafés and a beer hall serving excellent food. Open from 10am.

Maison Charlotte € *Mittelstrasse 20, 14467 Potsdam, tel: 0331 200 0536.* There's an excellent choice of places to eat and drink in Potsdam's charming Holländisches Viertel/Dutch Quarter, none more inviting than this French-style bistro. Open noon–11pm.

HAMBURG AND THE NORTH

BALTIC COAST

Fischmarkt €–€€ *Strandpromenade 33, 18609 Ostseebad Binz, tel: 038393 38 14 43.* Widely held to be the best place to eat in Rügen Island's elegant resort of Binz, the restaurant of the Hotel Lissek serves local and international dishes, featuring the freshest of fish.

Käpt'n Nemo €–€€ *Strandpromenade 1, 17424 Heringsdorf, tel: 038378 288 17.* The pier in Usedom Island's premier resort of Heringsdorf offers budget dining in the 'Nauticus', while fine seafood dishes can be enjoyed in this net-bedecked establishment.

BREMEN

Ratskeller € *Rathaus, Am Markt, 28195 Bremen, tel: 0421 321676.* North German specialities in a characterful atmosphere. The extent of the wine list is almost beyond belief. Also here is the far more refined, award-winning international restaurant, L'Orchidée.

HAMBURG

Fischereihafen €€ *Grosse Elbstrasse 3, 22767 Hamburg, tel: 040 381816.* Be sure to book your table well in advance; popular modern fish restaurant serving freshwater and seafood specialities.

Old Commercial Room €€ *Englische Planke 10, 20459 Hamburg, tel: 040 36 63 19.* Seafood restaurant by the Michaelis-Kirche with a maritime atmosphere. Try *Labskaus*, the traditional seaman's dish.

ROSTOCK-WARNEMÜNDE

Gartenlaube € *Anastasiastrasse 24, 18119 Rostock-Warnemünde, tel: 0381 526 61.* Charming little establishment, with friendly service and a good range of regionally inspired dishes changed daily.

WISMAR

Alter Schwede € *Am Markt 20, 23966 Wismar, tel: 03841 283552.* On Wismar's main square, this is the Hansa town's oldest building, full of atmosphere in which to enjoy satisfying traditional food.

DRESDEN AND THE TWO SAXONYS

DESSAU

Kornhaus € *Kornhausstrasse 146, 06846 Dessau, tel: 0340 640 4141.* On the banks of the Elbe on the northwestern outskirts of the city, this restaurant is one of the key buildings in Dessau's Modernist heritage. The hearty food makes much use of fresh local ingredients.

DRESDEN

Coselpalais € *An der Frauenkirche 12, 01067 Dresden, tel: 0351 496 2444.* Rebuilt baroque palace offering refined French and German cuisine in an elegant setting. Its Grand Café is the place to come for superlative coffee and cakes.

Italienisches Dörfchen € *Theaterplatz 3, 01067 Dresden, tel: 0351 498160.* There is solid Saxon food in the Kurfürstenzimmer, Italian cuisine in the Bellotto, and delicious cakes in the patisserie.

LEIPZIG

Auerbachs Keller € *Mädlerpassage, Grimmaische Strasse 2–4, 04109 Leipzig, tel: 0341 216 100.* Atmospheric vaulted cellars and one of the best places to dine in town, serving a mixture of carefully prepared Saxon and international dishes at very reasonable prices.

Stadtpfeifer €€€ *Augustusplatz 8, 04109 Leipzig, tel: 0341 217 8920.* Set in the modern building of the Gewandhaus, home of the renowned orchestra. Gourmet food of the utmost refinement.

MEISSEN

Vincenz Richter € *An der Frauenkirche 12, 01662 Meissen, tel: 03521 453285.* Charming and popular 16th-century wine tavern that is the place to come to enjoy refined versions of traditional Saxon cooking and to sample the surprisingly good local wines.

WEIMAR AND THURINGIA

WEIMAR

Zum Zwiebel € *Teichgasse 6, 99423 Weimar, tel: 03643 502375.* An unpretentious establishment serving up those traditional Thuringian specialities (notably the region's famous sausages) that make other Germans smack their lips in anticipation.

HANOVER AND THE HARZ

GOSLAR

Andechser im Ratskeller € *Markt 1, 386406 Goslar, tel: 05321 392090.* Hearty Bavarian-style food beneath the vaults of the 15th-century town hall cellar.

HAMELIN

Kartoffelhaus im Bürgerhaus € *Kupferschmiedestrasse 13, 31785 Hameln, tel: 05151 22383.* Housed in one of Hamelin's historic town mansions, the 'Potato House' serves straightforward traditional fare in its individually styled dining rooms.

HANOVER

Georgenhof-Stern €€€ *Herrenhäuser Kirchweg 20, 30167 Hannover, tel: 0511 702244.* Close to the Herrenhausen Gardens and run by renowned chef and food writer Heinrich Stern. Delicious specialities include rack of lamb from Lüneburg Heath. The Georgenhof is also a charming, intimate hotel.

LÜNEBURG

Zum Heidkrug €–€€ *Am Berge 5, 21335 Lüneburg, tel: 04131 241 60.* A harmonious atmosphere reigns in the gourmet restaurant of the 15th-century Zum Heidekrug hotel, which specialises in contemporary German and Mediterranean cuisine, complemented by an exceptional choice of wines. Closed Sun and Mon.

QUEDLINBURG

Weinstube €–€€ *Romantik Hotel am Brühl, Billungstrasse 11, 06484, Quedlinburg, tel: 03946 9610.* Stylish food served in the charming wine cellar of one of Quedlinburg's most attractive hotels, best accompanied by wines from the nearby Saale-Unstrut region.

COLOGNE, THE RUHR AND RHINE

COLOGNE

Hausbrauerei Päffgen € *Friesenstrasse 64–66, 50670 Köln, tel: 0221 13 54 61.* Cologne is famous for *Kölsch*, the fresh and hoppy beer brewed in places like this century-old establishment with its own beer hall, where hearty regional food complements the drink.

Heising und Adelmann €€ *Friesenplatz 58–60, 50670 Köln, tel: 0221 130 94 24.* Trendy establishment serving creative international cuisine. Long bar, terrace and beer garden.

DÜSSELDORF

Zum Schiffchen € *Hafenstrasse 5, 40213 Düsseldorf, tel: 0211 132422.* An Altstadt institution, the 'Little Ship' combines cheerful beer-hall atmosphere with generous portions of hearty food.

RHINE VALLEY

Zum Schiffen € *Am Rhein 4, 56321 Rhens, tel: 02628 22 16.* The 'Ship' specialises in regional dishes featuring fish and game, served in an upper-floor dining room or terrace overlooking the Rhine.

SOUTHWEST TO THE BLACK FOREST

BADEN-BADEN

Zum Alde Gott €€€ *Weinstrasse 10, 76534 Baden-Baden-Neuweier, tel: 07223 572 36.* Under the direction of an acclaimed chef, this award-winning establishment offers diners regional and international specialities based firmly on seasonal produce.

FRANKFURT

Main Tower Restaurant €€–€€€ *53rd floor, Neue Mainzer Strasse 52, 60297 Frankfurt-am-Main, tel: 069 36 50 47 77.* Dine in great style off international cuisine 200m (660ft) up at the top of the skyscraper home of the Bundesbank.

Zum Gemalten Haus € *Schweizer Strasse 67, 60594 Frankfurt-am-Main, tel: 069 614559.* One of the best places to sample tasty and filling local specialities washed down with *Äppelwoi* (cider).

FREIBURG

Colombi-Hotel €€€ *Rotteckring 16, 79098 Freiburg im Breisgau, tel: 0761 210 60.* Freiburg's leading hotel offers a choice of three restaurants, ranging from a cosy *Weinstube* to an award-winning establishment run by one of Germany's most acclaimed chefs.

HEIDELBERG

Schlossweinstube €€ *Schlosshof, 69117 Heidelberg, tel: 06221 979 70.* Stylish dining in Heidelberg's Castle, where contemporary design complements the historic atmosphere. Evenings only.

KONSTANZ

Siber €€€ *Seestrasse 25, 78464 Konstanz, tel: 07531 996 69 90.* Michelin-starred gourmet restaurant, part of an intimate hotel in an elegant Art Nouveau villa. Terrace with lake views.

STUTTGART

Harris Kachelofen € *Eberhardstrasse 10, 80173 Stuttgart, tel: 07071 929 40.* A city-centre institution, serving traditional Swabian specialities. Deservedly popular.

MUNICH AND THE SOUTH

AUGSBURG

Die Ecke € *Elias-Holl-Platz 2, 86150 Augsburg, tel: 0821 51 06 00.* Cheerful bistro offering Swabian and Bavarian dishes.

BERCHTESGADEN

Bräustüberl € *Brauhausstrasse 13, Berchtesgaden, tel: 08652 97 67 24.* Brewery restaurant dishing up unpretentious but very satisfying Alpine food from Bavaria and nearby Austria.

MUNICH

Augustiner € *Neuhauserstrasse 27, 80331 München, tel: 089 2318 3257.* Wholesome Bavarian dishes served to 1,000-plus diners at a time in its spacious beer hall.

Dallmayr €€–€€€ *Dienerstrasse 14–15, 80331 München, tel: 089 213 5100.* Delicatessen with an elegant restaurant serving fine food made from the freshest ingredients.

Pfistermühle €–€€ *Pfisterstrasse 4, 80331 München, tel: 089 2370 3865.* Refined Bavarian cuisine complemented by an excellent selection of Franconian and other wines.

Weisses Bräuhaus € *Tal 7, 80331 München, tel: 089 29 01 38.* Authentic Munich inn with lots of atmosphere, a mixed clientele, and heaps of hearty meat-based dishes from its own slaughterhouse.

NUREMBERG AND NORTHERN BAVARIA

NUREMBERG

Goldenes Posthorn €€–€€€ *Glöckleinsgasse 2, 90403 Nürnberg, tel: 0911 22 51 53.* Atmospheric 500-year-old establishment. The succulent Franconian dishes have won countless awards.

REGENSBURG

Historische Wurstküche € *Thundorferstrasse 3, 93047 Regensburg, tel: 0941 59 098.* An essential stop for anyone in town. The menu: sausages and more sausages – but what sausages! The sauerkraut is the real thing too.

INDEX